L_OST + FOUND

Finding Myself by Getting Lost in an Affair

David Trotter
Afterword by Laura Trotter

nurmal
resources to inspire a new normal

Published in the United States by Nurmal Resources.
www.nurmal.com

Library of Congress Control Number: 2010910980

ISBN-13 9781935798019
ISBN-10 1935798014

Printed in the United States of America

Design and layout by 8TRACKstudios
www.8TRACKstudios.com

Cover photo by David Trotter
Author photo by Shauntelle Sposto

For Laura
who has been willing to forgive
my darkest moments when I was lost
and invest in the new partnership
that we've found together.

I love you.

CONTENTS

PREFACE

"Lost + Found" is my story, and it is told from my vantage point…the only one I have. As I anxiously typed each word, I was thankful for the challenge I heard from Anne Lamott years ago at a writer's workshop.

"Your story is yours to tell, and no one can stop you.
Tell it like it happened!"

Rather than sanitize my experience, I have chosen to tell it as I remember it. My desire is that you will experience the highest 'highs' and the lowest 'lows' as I search for the life I always wanted. In my opinion, the power of my redemption is fully experienced against the backdrop of the depravity of my search.

I've done my best to capture the essence of each experience and conversation, and I have used actual journal entries, emails, blog posts, and letters as I recount this period of my life. Because of the nature of my story, I have changed the names of most individuals to avoid offense or embarrassment.

I'm honored to share my journey with you as a gift, and my hope (and prayer) is that it transforms you in some way.

- If you are in a dark season of life or if you encounter one in the future, may this story provide you with a small glimmer of light.

- If your partner has strayed, may you be filled with hope for the future.

- If you have been severely disappointed by someone, may you be filled with compassion for them in their brokenness.

- If you're simply a voyeur looking in on a train wreck, may you see that life is filled with possibilities.

- If you think something like this could never happen to you, think again.

- If you find yourself lost or stuck like I was, may you draw strength from the One who wrote my story of redemption.

May your heart be open along the journey.

David Trotter
Lakewood, California
July 2010

DYING TO QUIT

chapter one

As the chair slowly reclined, my heart began to race like that of a lamb led to slaughter. I gripped the padded arms of the chair and stared intently at the photos of his children as they gazed back at me from the wall. The muscles in my legs began to tighten, and I could feel perspiration forming on my forehead. I was straining to get out of there, but we hadn't even gotten started yet.

I was in the chair of my orthodontist.

Normally, my experience at his office was quite pleasant. Unlike the first time I had braces as a prepubescent tween, I actually enjoyed the process. The two ladies at the front counter were more than happy to make my appointments, and his assistants who did most of the work on me were gentle and always interested in what I was up to. On top of that, he was comping all the work, because I was...*his pastor.*

Humbling for sure.

When someone gives me a gift because of my role in their life, it is both encouraging and awkward at the same time. In this case, it had become painful.

As his 6' 4" frame hovered over me, his greeting was followed by two large hands heading straight for my mouth. My fear was that he would use his repertoire of ortho tools to slowly dismantle my teeth one by one or tighten my braces to the point that everything simply collapsed into my throat. My mind was running wild with fear that he was on to us.

Does he know?
Is he blind?
How can he not know?

Thank God he didn't talk that much. Adjustments were made, small talk was exchanged, and I was almost out of there. Hopefully, my anxiety and accompanying sweaty pits were not showing. All I had to do was check in at the front desk and get out the door.

As I was making my obligatory next appointment (which would be rendered meaningless within days), I noticed that he was lingering aimlessly in the lobby. Checking his Blackberry over and over nervously, he just stood there, and I was getting freaked out.

"Crap! He's waiting for me," I screamed in my head.

As I turned to walk out the front door, I felt his presence coming close from behind. I was preparing for the worst, but I wasn't quite sure what to do. As he called my name, my fists clinched, and I was ready.

"If he takes a swing, dodge it, and take your best shot," I kept telling myself.

"David, I just wanted to let you know…"
He held back with a pregnant pause.

"Yeah?"

"I just want to let you know that I'm happy for you that you're taking a sabbatical," he said graciously. "I'll be praying for you for sure."

"Um...thanks Ben...I...appreciate that," I stumbled through my words.

My fists unclenched, but my butt cheeks didn't. As he headed back in, I bolted for my car with cell phone in hand. I double-clicked the call button and re-dialed her number.

"Hello?" she answered after the first ring.

"Hey."

"Are you okay? Did he say anything?"

"Hell, yes! Of course he said something! He said he is *praying* for me... what the heck?!?"

She burst into laughter at the shock of his words and his cluelessness of what was impending.

"He didn't ask you any questions? Or pry about anything?" she asked.

"Thank God no. I'm so glad *that's* over," I said. "He has no clue what's coming...are you ready to tell him?"

I Would Have Never Imagined
A month prior, I would have never imagined that I'd fall in love with my orthodontist's wife...

...who was also my wife's best friend.

It all started in the months leading up to a two-week mission trip to southern India. Although I had travelled to India on multiple occasions, this team was being led by one of our staff pastors and three leaders who had joined me on each previous humanitarian trip. Their leadership freed me up to relax a bit and play more of a pastoral role within our team of 17 men and women. We had so many wonderful things planned including a children's vacation bible school, water well dedications, food distribution, and many more projects that would make Mother Theresa smile with pride.

As the trip started to draw near, I found myself becoming more and more weary from 10 years of full-time ministry…five of which had been spent starting a new church in the communities surrounding Long Beach, a multi-ethnic city in southern California. What was glamorous in the beginning had become a brutal grind with over 70 hours invested weekly in much of what Jesus probably never envisioned.

I'll never forget the first time I saw her…Samantha that is.

Our church was about a year old, and we were meeting in the "fellowship hall" of the congregation that helped us get started. With 100 or so people showing up every Sunday, it was easy to notice when visitors were present. I would usually head straight toward them after the service to connect as best as I could and make them feel welcome in the hopes that they would come back the next week. Without butts in the seats, there would be no offering in the box…which meant that I would eventually quit being able to feed my own kids.

On this particular Sunday, we mixed up the seating arrangement. Instead of the traditional rows, we set up large round tables with eight chairs wrapped around them. I can't even remember the topic of the morning, but I do remember that one of the founding couples from the church was moving to Utah the next week.

As was our tradition, we loved to bring the family up front, pray for them, and bless them in their new journey. As I brought up Sal and Mary, I was in my usual post-service, wacky mood that lent itself to off-handed comments that I sometimes wanted to suck back into the recesses of my brain.

"So, you guys are moving to Utah?" I asked.

"Yes, it's for Sal's job, and we're really looking forward to it," Mary was so proud.

"That's right...you're not moving there just so Sal can have an extra wife," I clarified.

The crowd burst into laughter...some genuine and some filled with nervousness. In my ignorance, I had not thought of the impact on someone from a Mormon background...or someone who was married to a pseudo-Mormon.

That was Samantha.

After being given a heads-up by one of my leaders that a first-time visitor had commented at her table about hating churches that ripped on Mormons, I rushed to find her as she picked up her kids from the children's program. Thank God her husband wasn't there.

As I nervously apologized and backed my way out of my own stupidity, she was quite gracious in accepting my apology. That day began a unique attraction that slowly percolated for four years in my heart until it bubbled up in the weeks prior to our mission trip to India.

Samantha was going with us.

As satisfaction for my life waned, my curiosity about Samantha increased. My mind began to wander..."Wow, she'll be on the trip...I wonder what that will be like. Will we talk? Will we connect? Will it turn into something?"

I started thinking more and more about her as the days approached. It was a mixture of excitement for her to have the life-changing opportunity to make an impact in India combined with an attraction to her as a woman I was interested in spending time with.

I wasn't consumed, but I was definitely curious.

Since our flight was scheduled on Sunday at midnight, we planned to gather in the parking lot of one of three church locations we had started. As everyone circled up to pray, I shared a few words of encouragement for both the team members and the nervous families who had shown up to send us off.

After a brief prayer, I turned to Ben (my orthodontist), "You gotta know that Samantha will never be the same after this trip. She's going to have experiences in India that will change her life, and you better be ready for it."

"I know...I know," he nervously responded.

Why the hell did I say that? I'm not sure if it was a prophetic message, utter stupidity, or an ironic warning from God. Others would later see it as predatory, but we'll get to that.

The truth is...I was right. She *would* be different...and so would I.

I *wanted* something different. I was sick and tired of life as I knew it. I had ended up with an existence that I didn't want any more. The problem was that I had chosen it myself. I had chosen the life I was living.

From Kentucky to California...But Not Back

Having grown up in Kentucky, my family and I made the cross-country move to California in between my sophomore and junior years in high school in order to start a new church. Despite the brutality of moving away from the community in which I had grown up since first grade, I was at least popular during that last month of school.

I was moving to California!

This is every high schooler's dream if you live in Kentucky. California is the land of Hollywood, beaches, and babes.

Unfortunately, we moved to Lodi.

Let's just say that I didn't write home to tell anyone that there were no beaches and no babes. If you haven't been to Lodi, there are fields and cows and grapes...lots and lots of grapes. It was the most Kentucky-version of California my family could find...just my luck!

My dad worked for the government at the time, and they granted his request for a transfer to northern California. It was the place my mom and dad sensed a calling to begin a new church, which would end up starting toward the end of my senior year in high school. There was some sort of mystical draw to that part of the US since my dad had completed his high school years in the bay area as the son of a career Navy father.

With a howling, one-eyed cat named Dandy and a frequently-pooping mutt named Topper, we moved, I survived (barely), and my parents did their best to support me in my talents.

During my freshman year of high school in Kentucky, I had enrolled in a journalism class that crafted the school newspaper and yearbook. After a couple of weeks, there was a call for photographers, and it sounded somewhat interesting to me. I begged my grandparents for a camera for Christmas, and a Minolta x-370 showed up under the tree.

My journalism teacher invested in me hours of training over the course of the next year and half as she saw my natural ability. By my sophomore year, she was grooming me to take over the photo department for my last two years in high school. When I told her that I was moving to California, she was absolutely livid. Unfortunately, her investment wouldn't benefit her program any longer...but it did benefit me in the long run.

After settling in to our temporary housing in California and having our car stereo stolen within a week, my mom and I started the arduous task of looking for a high school for me to attend...not a private one...but a public high school with the very best photojournalism department we could find. That's right. My parents placed the priority on me being able to continue my learning in the area of photography rather than living in a particular town that they would prefer.

We travelled from school to school in Modesto, Manteca, Stockton, and eventually Lodi to interview journalism teachers. After gasping for air in Modesto and Manteca because of the local "agriculture" and dodging bullets in Stockton, we found our way onto the campus of Tokay High School in Lodi. We were greeted by an unassuming Asian man named "Woo"…Mr. Woo to those who didn't know him very well.

He was extraordinary. He welcomed me with his shiny bald head and his short, open arms, took a look at my portfolio, and invited me to attend a summer yearbook camp in Santa Cruz. As we walked out of his classroom, the decision had been made.

We were moving to Lodi!

Not quite what I had envisioned when we were making the five-day trek across the US…but it would do.

After a rough start trying to figure out how to dress and speak like someone from California, I finally quit saying "golly" and "fixin'" and all the things that would provoke laughter out of my new classmates. I played into the hick persona for a while as I gained my footing, but I was soon able to hold my own on the basketball court as the token white guy and in the darkroom with my photographic skills.

Over the next two years, I won a number of awards for my work, I started working for a local newspaper, and we also started attending a local church.

I had never really gone to a *real* church over the course of my life. I ventured inside one from time to time, but we weren't regular attenders. You see I grew up in Kentucky in what's called a "house church"…otherwise known as a church that meets in a house. My parents and I were part of a network of house churches that met all over the US, and that's all I had really ever known.

I saw my parents model close relationships with other couples, and I had great friendships with the other kids. As the adults sang, prayed, and listened to the pastor speak, I'd sit quietly on the floor of the living room looking at the maps in my Bible or making handprints in the shag carpet.

As we started to attend this new church in Lodi, kids from the youth group would beg me to come to their event every week. What they didn't realize is that I was too cool for that. I was a photographer, *and* I was on the basketball team. They were just lame kids carrying their pleather-covered Bibles to youth group while cool kids were out doing something fun…which would be pretty much anything other than church.

I finally relented one Tuesday night, and I showed up. I drove my cool, cream station wagon into the church parking lot, and I nervously headed into the similarly colored building. Within minutes, I found myself getting sucked into a frenetic game of "capture the flag"…otherwise known as "chase the cute girls."

Within a couple of weeks, I was attending every Tuesday night, and I quickly noticed something different about these kids…especially two guys named Brian and Damon. They were seniors, and they were passionate about "Jeeesuuus" as they called him. They did stuff that I hadn't ever thought of…like they read the Bible and prayed in "tongues" (a crazy-sounding language that's supposed to be just between you and God) and raised their hands while we sang songs. Weird stuff for sure!

One February evening, the youth pastor invited anyone up front who wanted to follow "Jeeesuuus", and he started praying for everyone. As my heart began pounding out of my chest, I knew he was talking to me. Sure, I had grown up in a Christian home, been baptized, and followed all the "rules"…but this was different.

I walked up front, and Brian and Damon were there to pray for people. I looked at the pastor and said, "I want something different. I want what they have."

Tears began to stream down my pimply face, and I felt like something had changed that evening. I felt something…God, I think. Although I was a pretty straight and narrow kid, I liked this whole idea of "living for Jesus" and helping others experience that, too.

I immediately started wearing Jesus shirts to school including the one
with Buddha on a cross and some sort of "your god didn't die for you"
phrase emblazoned on the front. With my Bible in hand and cross around
my neck, I was making looooots of friends.

Within the next year, I found myself on a plane with 15 or so other
kids heading to Dallas, Texas, for a youth convention. The climax of the
multi-day event was a giant 10,000 kid "church meeting" in the convention center to ring in the new year...1991.

At the beginning of the conference, I noticed a fresh-out-of-bible-college
"salesman" who would stand at the front door and pass out literature trying to get kids to come to their school. Since I had already been accepted
into the photojournalism department at Western Kentucky University, I
had no interest whatsoever in some unaccredited bible college.

Day after day, we would enter the doors, and I'd notice the same guy
over and over. By the end of the three days, my ears were filled with the
speakers' words, and my heart was overflowing with questions about the
future. I started to wonder if a bible college was right for me.

On the final evening, it was like a replay from that night a year before at
my church's youth group. The pastor asked us if we were committed to
"go" anywhere God wanted us to go. If we were, he invited us to come
down to the floor of the convention center and pray. As more and more
kids streamed down the stairs, I found my legs moving toward the aisle.
It was as if my heart had bypassed my head, and I was going down to
that floor whether I liked it or not.

As I kneeled on the ice-cold, concrete floor of the giant convention center with hundreds of other sweaty, puberty-induced teenagers, I knew
what God was calling me to do.

I knew I wasn't supposed to go back to Kentucky. I knew I wasn't supposed to be a Sports Illustrated photographer like I thought.

God was calling me to be…*a pastor.*

I knew it deep within.
I didn't tell anyone that night, but I knew it…and that's all that mattered.

After making the flight back home, I dropped my bags, and my parents asked the obligatory question, "How was the trip?"

"Fine," I muttered as I moped down the hallway.

After a few minutes, I emerged from my room and plopped down on the living room couch. I could feel the tears starting to well up in nervous anticipation of my parent's reaction. I did my best to suck the salty drops back in, but it didn't work. With sniffling and snorting between each word, I blubbered through it, "I don't think…I'm supposed to…go back to Kentucky…I think I'm supposed to be a…pastor."

As tears streamed down my face, my parents started to laugh.
"What? Why are you laughing at me?" I asked in confusion.

"We thought this might be where your life would take you, but we didn't want to push you in to something," my dad reassured. I began to see my parents eyes fill with understanding.

Wow. How could they have known?
Amazing stuff for a kid to hear, huh?

Hot Pink Shorts and a Golden Mane
After promptly calling my would-be roommate in Kentucky to let him in on the bad news, I started researching colleges on the west coast. I arranged a week long tour of four possible choices, and I hit the road during a break due to year-round school. Although it was the farthest from home, I chose Southern California College…now called Vanguard University. It was a quaint school of 1,000 or so students at the time, and the kids seemed to be less weird than at the other places.

In the Fall of 1991, I moved to southern California to start my schooling. I tried to find my way among the myriad of paths toward full-time ministry…which was the ultimate "goal."

Maybe music?
"No, I can't carry a tune."

How about children's ministry?
"Nah…too many snotty noses. Maybe youth ministry would be better… they're already potty trained!"

After a summer internship at a local church that included me leading music on a guitar with the only three chords I knew and teaching a bunch of squirrelly kids about Jesus' love, I soon discovered that youth ministry was actually for someone who loves youth…which didn't include me.

As an 'only child,' I started to think, "I haven't hung out with kids most of my life, so why would I start now?" Jesus may love them, but I found them to be a pain in the ass. Who would've guessed?

Although I was disinterested in music, kids, and youth…the three primary on-ramps to full-time ministry in the church world, I did have a couple of professors who saw my potential…and one who thoroughly discouraged me from ever going into ministry. But, he's dead now… which has nothing to do with any of this, but I thought you should know.

As I showed up on campus for my sophomore year, I found myself on the 5th floor once again. In the first week, we were herded into an outing with our sister floor from the adjacent tower where most of the "laaaadies" lived. We were allowed into each other's rooms once a week…as long as the door was left open a Bible-length or more and everyone kept their clothes on…and didn't dance. In the conservative, Christian college world, closed doors lead to dancing, which soon leads to sex. Not sure how that happens, but that's what Jesus said…somewhere…according to the denomination.

As we circled up, I immediately noticed a pair of hot pink shorts to my left...the bright color that is...not the booty inside them. As my eyes made their way upward, I was overcome by the brilliance of the shiny, golden mane of a female who I had never laid eyes on. She wasn't like the other "girls" who bent over the ice cream trough in the cafeteria... she was a "woman."

Her name was Laura Hatcher.
She transferred in as a junior, but I knew she was *way* out of my league.

We played a little game of hide and seek that night, and as soon as they said "go", I went chasing after the new gal. I never did catch up to her that evening, but I did later in the year.

Mid-way through the semester, we found ourselves commiserating together over the fact that our "relationships" weren't working out. The more we talked...the more potential I saw. I thought I might actually have a shot.

"Um...ya know...um...the junior / senior banquet is coming up, and... um...I am going to be taking photos...aaaannnd...I was thinking...you may not be interested...but would you maybe like to go with me?"

"I'd love to!" she responded.

"Holy crap!" I thought in my head, but responded with a simple..."cool."

The next night, we went out on our first date...dinner and a walk on the beach. I kissed her, and we went out every single night for three weeks straight. I don't know where the heck I got the money, but I found it... and she was worth every penny.

After three weeks, I couldn't contain myself any more.

"Laura...I love you...and I want to marry you," I said with a deep exhale.

Let's just say that her response wasn't exactly what I had hoped for. She just sat there, and the junior/senior banquet (a week later) ended up being a nightmare. As part of the big event, we went to Disneyland all day, and the actual banquet was at night. She ignored me, flirted with other guys, and essentially broke my heart.

After dropping her off at her dorm, I remember sitting in my green, Honda hatchback with gray, furry seats. With the same, blubbering voice I used a couple of years earlier, I called my parents on my over-sized Motorola flip phone, "I….think…I've…lost…her!"

My parents consoled me as best they could as I realized that I moved at the speed of light when the love of my college life was moving at a snail's pace. Okay…a snail's pace is a bit of an exaggeration. Maybe she was just normal.

School was out for the summer break, and we went our separate ways. She went to Yosemite for a biology class, and I headed to Alabama to connect with a pastor who was rumored to hear crazy stuff from God… and I was hoping he would hear something real good for me.

Thankfully, God came through for me in the form of a dream that Laura experienced while we were apart. She dreamed that we were getting married! Who knows if it was due to sleeping in a tent with frigid temperatures, but I frankly didn't care. I was just glad that she was seeing things my way. With her permission, I met with her father for his approval. After three months of dating, I got down on one knee and asked her hand in marriage…and most importantly, she said "yes!"

During my junior year and her senior, we planned a wedding…okay, *she* planned the wedding. I worked three jobs and packed in as many college credits as I could. Continuing in my driven fashion, I was the yearbook and newspaper photo editor, a teaching assistant for a professor, and a sales assistant at Nabisco…a fancy way of saying I stocked cookies and crackers three days a week.

Somehow, we managed to pull it all off and got married on May 14, 1994…one week after Laura graduated from college. We honeymooned in Boston in between the raindrops and then moved into married housing back on campus in Costa Mesa.

Over the next year, Laura completed her teaching credential at a different college, and I kept working three jobs as I finished up my credits for a BA and MA…all in four years. I could feel a drive within me to "walk the line twice" as I'd say. I wanted people to see me do what no other person was doing. I wanted to stand out ahead of the pack…and it almost killed me.

In fact, I *did* walk the line twice that spring…but I never finished my master's thesis…heck, I don't even remember what it was about. I got about two-thirds of the way through it and just sputtered out. I was done…burnt to a crisp. I didn't want to take any more damn photos or stock any more damn shelves of cookies or write another damn word about church.

I just wanted to be done…and actually begin working at a church. That's what I did all this for, *right?* To work at a church?

The only problem was that no one wanted to hire me. All my contacts were within the Assemblies of God denomination, because that's the type of college I attended. I went on a number of interviews, but it was apparent that I had no experience and asked *way* too many questions.

Dying to Get Started
While Laura took a job as a bilingual teacher in Santa Ana, I was recruited and hired at the largest paper distributor in the US. Soon, I was tethered by a headset to a curvy desk within a cubicle on the 6th floor of a fluorescent-lit, office building for eight hours a day helping *lovely* printers find the paper they desperately needed.

I often found myself lying in bed at night crying my way to sleep. *I* was the one who was desperate…desperate to see my hopes and dreams come to fruition. Had I really racked up all those student loans going through all that schooling and training to work at a paper company?

Since no one would hire me at a church, I did the only thing I knew…I went back to school. Because I didn't actually get the piece of paper for my MA, I wanted to have something to hang on my wall. I transferred my units to Fuller Theological Seminary and started driving from Orange County to Pasadena two days a week to complete a more extended masters program. The classes weren't that exciting, but at least I was doing something related to ministry…and the fried zucchini at the burger stand next to the college was pretty good, too.

By the spring of 1997, I had given up on pursuing a position at a church. I was resigned to just keep working at the paper company. A few months later…a previous professor from Vanguard gave me a call…not the one who's dead, but one who actually liked me.

"David, there's a guy in my class who's starting a church in Costa Mesa, and I want you to meet him. I think you guys would be great partners," he said.

Later that week, I found myself in a coffee shop wearing my standard corporate uniform of shirt and tie…waiting for this pastor to walk through the door. As I waited impatiently, I noticed a rough character walk in. With two large silver hoop earrings and long sideburns that framed his face, this guy came walking toward me in his black leather jacket and scuffed up biker boots.

"Hi, are you David?" he asked.

"Um…yeah." This couldn't be him…could it?

This "character" was actually the pastor of the new church, and his name was Kirk Parker. His rough exterior didn't exactly match my pre-conceived idea of what a pastor should look like, but his heart was filled with compassion for people in need. He had a vision to make a difference in the lives of people who lived in Costa Mesa, and he was looking for partners who would help him. Over the next hour, it was apparent that we were gelling in a unique way, and I was definitely interested in checking out this new church.

As the church launched in October of 1997, Laura and I showed up on the first day, and I immediately started volunteering. I could feel a passion and drivenness begin to emerge like I had never felt before. I had recovered from the burnout of three years prior, and I was raring to go. By February of 1998, I was finally hired as a full-time Associate Pastor at ROCKharbor Church.

I couldn't believe it. I was *finally* doing what I was called to do back on that cold, concrete, convention center floor seven years prior. I was doing it...but I had no idea what I was doing.

As the church grew to over 1,000 adults in the first year, I was in *way* over my head as I oversaw most of the ministries except the Sunday service and the finances. I made quite a few messes to say the least... including the first men's retreat where we went $7,500 in the hole. (The business guy still doesn't like me.)

Frankly, all that responsibility just wasn't enough.
I wanted to experience more.
I wanted to *lead* more.

Without looking back, I pushed and pushed to find what was missing in my life.

The next few years included...

- leaving ROCKharbor to start a ministry called THEOOZE,
- having our first child,
- going back on staff at ROCKharbor after depleting our savings,
- having two miscarriages,
- leaving ROCKharbor again to work at another church,
- getting fired from that church,
- and having our second child two weeks later.

After getting fired six months in at the new church, I was exasperated and essentially *pissed*. Who wouldn't be pissed? I left a comfortable position at ROCKharbor to work with this new congregation...banking on a promise that they'd help me start my *own* church within a couple of years.

Well, the Elder Board got their panties in a wad over some "Jackass-style" videos I produced for my website...paymystudentloan.com. Don't go looking for it, because it's not there anymore...although I do have copies of the videos if you ever want to watch them. They are brilliant! Unfortunately, the Board didn't exactly think so.

"David, these videos are a lack of judgment on your part, and they are incongruent with your role of Associate Pastor. We need to ask for your resignation," they said.

Let's just say that this didn't go over too well with my pregnant wife who was due within 2 weeks. My non-sinful, non-sexual, stupidity-laden videos were the impetus of me getting booted from my passion...ministry.

If you've ever been fired from a church, you'll know that there is no better time than the present to start a church of your own. It's a spiritual way of flipping the middle finger at the Elder Board who sent you packing... and uh...great way to help people know Jesus, too. Not that the former would be any part of *my* motivation, but I have seen that trait in other pastors from time to time.

Falling in Love With My First Mistress
So, that's exactly what we did...we started a new church in Long Beach which is about 30 minutes up the 405 freeway. It wouldn't have been possible without the incredible support of the pastor at El Dorado Park Community Church...Rob Mason. He was a cantankerous sort...and still is...but he's also one of the strongest people you'll ever meet. I don't mean in the "lift a car up on the curb" sort of way...I mean in his heart.

In traditional churches, there are often a handful of old stodgy people who have been sitting in the same pew their entire life, and they get pretty riled up when anything gets changed...especially if it involves a bunch of young people with loud music, black curtains, and glowing candles.

Those old people tried to push him around constantly, and he wouldn't have any thing to do with it. He pushed right back, and there's nothing more satisfying than having someone stand up for you when there's a pack of old people breathing down your neck. Thankfully, we started with 12 "young people" from the congregation...all in their 40s and 50s. They didn't know me, and I didn't know them.

Rob began a Sunday evening service a couple of years prior as an alternative to the hymn-laden, organ-playin', pew-sittin' service in the morning. Upon my arrival, the evening service was running around 30 people...almost half of which were over the age of 45...and the other half were under 15. Tough crowd to preach to for sure.

In early 2003, I began to connect with those 15 or so adults, and I started casting a vision for a new church. We didn't know what the name was going to be, but we *did* know that it would impact the communities surrounding Long Beach. Actually, I'm not sure *they* knew that. In a lot of ways, they were along for a ride they had never been on before.

Prior to this, I had been part of two previous church starts...one with my parents during my senior year of high school and then ROCKharbor in 1997. In reality, I had never been the guy leading the charge. It was exciting and overwhelming for sure.

The week before Easter 2003, we held the final Sunday evening service. We took Easter morning off, and the next week we began meeting on Sunday mornings to start rallying a launch team to help begin the new church.

In the next few months, Revolution Church would be born.

Frankly, I've never worked so hard in my life. The three jobs and 20+ credits during college paled in comparison to what would come.

We rallied as many volunteers as we could.

We hired a worship leader…who wore red sweat pants.
We launched a phone campaign to 30,000 households.
We designed a website, bulletins, and flyers.
We passed out promotional material door to door.
We gave away Revolution-branded water at shopping centers.
We wrote press releases and developed media kits.
We held barbecues in the park.
We baked cookies and passed them out door-to-door on our street.

…all in the name of Jesus.

I'm sure he was proud on one level (Jesus, that is), but I've got to think he was wondering what all the fuss was about. I actually wonder if he was thinking that quite often over the next five or so years.

If you've never started a church before, here's the non-spiritual, business agenda to the process. If you don't have enough butts in the seats on Sundays, you won't have enough money to pay the bills Monday through Friday…which happens to include your paycheck. And, if you don't have a cool enough website, promotional flyer, bulletin, ambience, band, and sermon, then people generally won't come back.

Challenge them so that they'll feel like they're growing, but don't challenge them too much or they'll move down the street to the less-challenging church.

That's just the process to get disenchanted Christians to join the team so that you can have a group of people paying the bills. Meanwhile, you'll need to start motivating those people who have been generally self-centered to start being "outward-focused" to actually love their neighbor and invite them to church…and maybe tell them about Jesus if you're lucky.

I know it sounds cynical, but it's the undercurrent in most churches. It's the man behind the curtain, and I bought into it. I spent 70-80 hours a week trying to perfect everything in the name of "excellence and relevance" so that people would show up on Sunday morning or at a midweek Life Group and want to keep coming back.

Don't get me wrong. I deeply wanted people to experience God's love, grace, and forgiveness, but somehow the business of "doing" church overcame me. I let her seduce me.

In retrospect...I actually ran headlong into her arms. She was voluptuous and tempting. I looked into her eyes, and I just knew she could satisfy my soul. My deep down craving for affection and love was calling out her name. I was convinced that she could heal what was broken within me. When I heard her whispering to me, I melted inside. Her scent caused my heart to leap out of my chest, and I wanted more. I wanted her. I needed her. I finally gave all that I had to her.

Ministry had become my mistress.

Over the course of five years, the vision would continue to expand as I pursued my mistress. We outgrew the meeting hall where we had started, and we began gathering on Sundays around the corner from my house at a local high school in Lakewood. This would require us to purchase two 20' trailers, and fill them with every conceivable form of equipment... sound, lighting, video, decorations, and tons of children's ministry paraphernalia. We amassed an army of volunteers to arrive on Sundays at 6am to set everything up, lead two services, and then tear everything back down.

It was an arduous task, but it was well worth it. We were seeing so many people come to church, follow Jesus, and get baptized. Marriages were restored, addictions were overcome, and great things were happening... but it wasn't enough.

It was *never* enough.

I always wanted more. I wanted to put on bigger and better community events. I wanted more people to show up on Sundays. I wanted more people to follow Jesus, volunteer, and give. I wanted more people to invite their friends. I wanted the church to grow even bigger...but it wasn't.

Okay...yes, it was growing...but not fast enough. Even though we were the largest church in the Long Beach area that had started in the last 15 years, it still wasn't enough. There was a craving...a drivenness...deep inside of me to keep growing.

I couched it all in the language of ministry...
"God is calling us to reach more people who don't yet know Him."
"There are people throughout this area in desperate need."
"Don't you want your neighbors to have what you have deep inside?"

In a lot of ways, that was all true. I did feel a love and compassion for people far from God...but my heart had been given to my mistress so my motives were less than pure.

After starting two more church locations...one in Downey and one on the campus of Cal State University Long Beach...and beginning to film a 25 minute teaching message to be shown in all three churches on Sundays, I was starting to wither.

The mistress who once held me close and whispered words of affirmation was becoming mute. She had lured me in with her tempting promises, but I now saw that she was nothing more than a wretched hag.

Volunteers were growing weary at each location. Our Downey church was losing money by the week, and the campus pastor was losing steam by the moment. I became hyper-focused on details with my staff, and they were being smothered under the pressure. By the summer of 2007, I was dying on the inside...and it was showing up on the outside as well.

"I just can't do this any more...I'm so tired," I told my leadership team.

They did their best to encourage me, but they were tired as well. Although we were staying afloat financially, the pressure of finances, staffing, three locations, and the discontent of a number of leaders was sucking the life out of my relationship with the mistress that I had once lusted after. Like an affair gone bad, the ecstasy of the foreplay and intercourse was gone, and all I was doing was dealing with the mess that our entanglement had birthed.

"I just want to get out of all this," I told myself. "But…how can I bail on the vision that I've been pumping into everyone?"

I was stuck.

Some people didn't think the messages had enough Bible in them. Other people didn't like the weekly teaching film that was being shown. 90% of the congregation was barely giving a dime to the ministry, and many people were simply weary.

With the biggest push I could muster into the Fall and Christmas of 2007, I could feel myself drying up. I was so parched that I was willing to drink almost anything. The mistress who I had fallen in love with wasn't quenching my thirst any longer. She was withholding her love, and I wanted her to lust after me even more.

Meanwhile, my marriage was feeling the repercussions of 10 years of ministry and the 70-80 hours a week I had invested in Revolution for the past five years. My wife and I lead a lifestyle that wasn't verbalized, but clearly understood…she would work and take care of the kids…while I focused on the church. Although she kept asking for my help, I didn't have anything to give…nor did I really want to.

There was no adrenaline rush in prepping dinner, helping with homework, or bathing the kids before bed. I'd rather sit on the couch with my computer answering "important" emails, updating the website, or prepping the next promotional campaign. I knew she was resigned to the fact that this was how our life and marriage was going to be. I was happy that she had finally quit nagging me.

In fact, we rarely even fought, and I actually thought that was a sign of a good marriage. I'd tell people, "Yeah, I don't even remember the last time we had a fight." On the other hand, I wasn't too happy that her affection was virtually non-existent. She was disconnected…but so was I.

In reality, we had become more like roommates with a long history of staying out of each other's way. I loved that there were no "honey do" lists. I thoroughly enjoyed my freedom to do whatever I wanted…whenever I felt like doing it. She knew that most Saturdays included message preparation and every Sunday was already booked solid. She had become a single Mom, and I didn't even realize it. What I did realize was my longing for love and partnership, and I wasn't getting what I truly wanted.

I felt all-alone. I was sick and tired of having to herd my staff. I was overwhelmed by the church finances. I was weary from pushing so hard for 5 years straight. And, on top of that, neither my mistress nor my wife was giving me what I wanted…affection.

I was dying to quit.

As our team of 17 boarded the plane to India, I noticed Samantha out of the corner of my eye. She had a sparkle in her smile as she anticipated the adventure to come. As she took her seat across the aisle from me, our eyes met momentarily.

I smiled back at her, and said, "Ready for an adventure?"

"Absolutely!"

Neither one of us knew how adventurous life would become.

chapter two

Packing for India is a monumental task that I usually wait to start until the day I leave. My wife rolls her eyes at me as I furiously make a list of all the items that I'll need.

In order of importance…snacks, laptop, iPod, camera, bug spray, Malaria pills, deodorant, underwear, toothbrush, toilet paper, wet wipes, long pants, button up shirts, flip flops, sleep sheet, travel pillow, water bottle, my Bible, and snacks. Did I mention lots and lots of snacks? For the sake of my relationship with our hosts, I eat a few bites of Indian food at each meal…pushing around the spicy curry concoction on my plate more than anything.

The first time I went to India I thought I'd "man up" and eat everything. I spent more time praying for myself while squatting over a hole in the ground than I did praying for the sick that actually live in India. At one point on that trip, I forgot my backpack full of wet wipes and toilet paper so I resorted to wiping with 40 rupees. Considering the Indian alterna-

tive of using my left hand with the bucket of water in the outhouse, I
thought it was a dollar well spent. That money is probably still sitting
up on the overhead window ledge in that outhouse somewhere in the
middle of nowhere.

With my hard-sided, duct tape-reinforced luggage and my over-stuffed
backpack with dangling water bottle and travel pillow, I was ready to
jump in the car. As we caravanned to LAX, my heart started beating
with anticipation. No matter how many times I go to India, there is both
excitement and intrepidation. My mind starts to dig deep into the recesses of my brain to access file upon file of images and experiences
from previous trips. I start to think about the wonderful people who have
turned from a mass of nameless faces to close friends who I'm excited
to see. At the same time, I also remember the smoky stench of trash as it
smolders in the heat of the day, and I'm reminded of the mosquito bites
that mysteriously show up overnight.

It's worth it though. It's worth the money and the distress...it's worth
it to see the positive impact we're making and the relationships we're
building year after year.

My mind also fills with anxiety about the team. On every single trip,
there are people that spin out...or at least annoy me to death. I start
wondering who's gonna be the whiner that can't handle the discomfort.
Who's gonna be the over-spiritual one who thinks every person in India
has a demon inside them? Who's gonna be the non-eater that disap-
pears during meal time? Who's gonna be the pouter who believes no one
cares about them? And, who's gonna try to lead the team...even though
they're not the leader?

Excitement and intrepidation. That's how every trip begins for me.

While the particulars of the trip were no different, there was a new twist:
I was burned out. A few months prior, we had launched our third location of Revolution Church, and I was feeling the pressure of leading a
growing congregation, creating interactive teaching films every week,
and dealing with the challenges of staffing and finances.

Frankly, I didn't realize how crispy I was.

Wanna Start an Orphanage?

No matter how burned out I got, I always had space within my mind to dream up something fresh and exciting. I was addicted to starting new things, and that's why launching new locations of the church was so invigorating. I dreamed of launching eight locations in the communities surrounding Long Beach, but I also dreamed of seeing campuses (as we called them) emerge around the world.

"What would it be like to start vibrant congregations that are all part of a network that shared the same DNA of Revolution?" I dreamed with my staff.

As I shared this vision with others, they often became glassy-eyed but went along with the idea anyway. Who doesn't want to be part of something exciting? Beyond the initial enthusiasm, the other thing I saw was a look of "Oh crap, what's he going to ask me to do now?" I generally ignored these looks and found myself pressing on.

In this case, it was no different.

"What if we started a location of Revolution in Chennai, India?" I asked our team. "Wouldn't that be amazing!?!"

The dream was to start an English-speaking location of our church, and the message would be presented via teaching film produced in the US or India each week. The campus pastor would be on our staff, and we'd support and encourage one another around the globe.

"And while we're at it, let's start an orphanage in the same city!" I dreamed. Most people were tired just trying to stay up with my brain. I know I was.

Having taken a scouting trip in the summer of 2007, we had learned quite a bit about planting a church in India. We also felt like it was somewhat premature. As an alternative, I decided that I wanted to start the orphanage as a first step. Instead of initiating this project through Revolution, I thought that our family could step forward and rally people to make it happen in partnership with Harvest India – the organization we've worked closely with for years.

My wife and I discussed the possibility of adding another couple to the mix so we wouldn't feel alone in the venture. After a few discussions about several families, we felt like we should invite Ben and Samantha to join us in the effort.

I chatted with both of them, and they were ecstatic to say the least.

While we were in India, the plan was for Samantha and I to research possible homes for the children to live in. We contacted our good friend Suresh Kumar who is the president of Harvest India, and he made arrangements for his staff to accompany us with a realtor.

After a 48-hour trip to India, the rest of the team boarded a train to head eight hours deeper into the country while three of us including myself, Samantha, and Michael (our Downey campus pastor) stayed behind.

We woke up the next morning and headed out on quite an adventure. Enjoying the comfort of an air-conditioned van, I began asking our translators a myriad of questions that flowed freely from my brain. We first ventured into a slum where our contacts had been working for a number of years. We walked through a ghetto with sewage flowing in open gutters, wild dogs roaming about, and school-aged children playing in the streets in the middle of the day.

"Why aren't these kids in school?" I asked.

"Their families don't have money to purchase uniforms or textbooks, so they can't attend," our translator explained in a thick accent that rivaled the guy who works at the 7-Eleven near my house.

Our sadness was increasing with the appearance of each child who followed us around like we were movie stars from America. They simply wanted to touch us and shake our hands, but instead they were finding their way into our hearts. I could see Samantha begin to tear up at one point, and my heart was drawn to her compassion.

I have to admit that I secretly wished Michael's 400-pound frame would just disappear. I wanted to experience all of this with *just* her, but it would have been awkward for us to stay behind alone.

Although we made a few good contacts, we just didn't find a home that was sufficient in size or quality for what we had in mind. We knew that we'd need to take another tour at the end of our trip before we boarded our plane to fly home.

The next day, we arrived at the train destined for Tenali – the headquarters of Harvest India. As we made our way on board, I was reminded of the unique scent that came along free of charge in the first class section…a mixture of Indian air freshener, air conditioning Freon, and the body odor of cooped-up passengers who don't believe in deodorant.

As we headed toward our assigned seating area, there were numerous seats wide open. Michael plopped down, and Samantha immediately sat next to him. I knew that something was going on in my heart when I felt a disappointment that she didn't sit next to me. It was like I was back at the middle school lunch tables hoping that the cute girl would head my way. Instead, she sat next to the fat kid who would keep her warm and make her laugh...all at the same time.

As the train ride dragged on and on, I moved over to the window seat and listened to the folksy tunes of Kimya Dawson. There was something raw and melancholy about her lyrics that drew me in.

"Whatcha listenin' to?" Samantha curiously asked.

"This gal named Kimya Dawson…amazin' stuff!" I said. "Here…listen to this."

I passed her one of my ear buds, and she popped it in for a listen. Every middle schooler's dream...to be sharing a song with a cute girl side-by-side. She jumped in midway through the bouncy tune...

> *So if you wanna burn yourself remember that I LOVE YOU.*
> *and if you wanna cut yourself remember that I LOVE YOU.*
> *and if you wanna kill yourself remember that I LOVE YOU.*
> *Call me up before your dead, we can make some plans instead.*
> *Send me an IM, I'll be your friend.* [1]

She laughed and ended up sticking around to chat.

I asked her how she was doing on the trip and about her hopes and dreams for our time in India. She talked about being excited to experience the culture and to have the opportunity to make a positive impact toward those who were hurting.

As we began to share about our lives back home as well, she curiously asked me about leading the church. She wanted to know what it was like. She wanted to know about me.

"It's harder than it looks. I mean...I get up on Sunday and get everyone excited...but I'm pretty overwhelmed." It felt good to confess to someone who genuinely cared.

"Really? I would've never known," she acted surprised.

"I know. Most people don't. I constantly feel like I'm not doing enough and that whatever I *am* doing isn't all that great."

I went on to share about the financial challenges of leading a church, the people that bitch and moan, and my own insecurities. She listened intently and stared at me with her big, beautiful, blue eyes. She began to pour courage into me.

"I think you're an amazing leader, and I know that God has called you to lead Revolution," she gushed. "Your messages are fabulous, you're fun to be with, and I love your heart for India."

"Really?" I was begging for more affirmation.

"Absolutely! You are an amaaaaazing man."

My parched heart got a taste of the nourishment I was dying for. I felt like she had breathed life into me, and I secretly wanted more. Yet, as we rejoined the team, my mind began to focus on the task at hand. Our team was there for one purpose…to serve the people of India.

Church Meetings, Demons, and Tears
On each of our mission trips, Harvest India sets up the entire agenda for our time, and they pack it full of activities. At each venue, we gain a better understanding of the ministry, and they give us an opportunity to participate as well.

> We hand out food to HIV/AIDS patients.
> We pray for the sick at medical camps in rural villages.
> We see the work of former prostitutes as they make purses.
> We play with hundreds of kids at multiple orphanages.
> We tour properties that are under construction.
> And, we see specifically where our resources are being put to use.

It's their way of showing us that they *really* do use all the money we invest in the projects that they were intended for.

We also attend local church services on Sunday. As we divide into two or three teams, we divvy up musically inclined team members so we minimize our embarrassment level as the native Indians sit and stare at us. We choose the speaker for the day and those who will share briefly about their relationship with God…called a 'testimony' in Christian circles.

On that hot, Sunday morning, we loaded into one of Harvest India's musty vans and headed out on the 30-minute, dirt-road drive to church. Wearing our finest saris and punjabis, our team of six was fired up to lead the morning service.

As we slowed to a stop and the dust settled, we saw a whitewashed, one-room, concrete church and heard the sound of drums playing over the loudspeaker mounted on a nearby pole. Someone from inside began calling out on the mic for the surrounding village to join in on the service. The blaring sounds were deafening and yet heart-warming all at the same time.

We stepped out of our shoes at the front door and stepped inside to find a crowd of women and a few men sitting on the tiled floor with an aisle up the center. Our team was welcomed to the stage where ubiquitous white plastic chairs lined the front wall and faced the congregation. We placed our backpacks under our seats and joined in the native songs as we faced the people...and they stared back.

Having sung in this circumstance on numerous occasions, the power of it all had waned a bit for me personally. In stark contrast, the first-timers on our team were overcome with the magnitude of the moment.

Here is the reality of the experience. We are sitting on a miniscule stage in a tiny church with 100+ villagers standing on a hardened floor in the middle of India worshipping God in two different languages and surrounded by mud floor, thatch-roofed huts. We would fly home in a few days and return to our lives filled with entertainment and excess while they continued to work in the fields to survive each day.

As the Indian music team continued to play, our team sat down and began to pray for the service. I was soon nudged by one of our team members as they pointed toward Samantha.

"Dave, is she okay?" Louis asked with a worried look on his face.

Louis was a relatively new follower of Jesus...and my neighbor back home. My wife and I met him a couple of years prior as a result of passing out freshly baked cookies door to door on our street. His wife and family eventually came to Revolution, experienced tremendous healing in their marriage, and were beginning to take on leadership roles. Yet, he had *never* seen anything like this.

As I observed Samantha's passionate praying, I noticed that her face was starting to turn red as sweat began to form on her brow. She was rocking back and forth and looking quite upset. My spiritual radar was turned up to high, but I couldn't get a read on the situation.

"Is this some sorta encounter with God?" I wondered to myself. "Or, is she goin' psycho...or even demonic?"

I wasn't quite sure, but I thought I should move in to assess the situation. As I traded seats with someone, I sat down next to her and began to pray. I placed my hand on her shoulder as a re-assuring touch, and she continued to pray even more violently.

At this point, I started to feel a bit awkward about this scene in front of the Indian congregation.

"What the heck? They put us up here on this stage, and now Samantha is freaking out!" I muttered to myself.

Her intensity level continued to rise. She was rocking back and forth aggressively, sweating profusely, and praying louder and louder. At just about the moment when I was going to lead her off the stage, she abruptly grabbed my hand from her shoulder and said, "Stop praying for me! Stop it!"

I'm thinking, "Helloooo!?! We've got a problem on our hands."

With her eyes tightly closed, she called out for the other team members, "Pray for him. Don't pray for me. Pray for him now!"

As they all willingly started to join in, I sat there wondering what was happening. I wasn't sensing any sort of spiritual moment...good, bad, or ugly. The whole scene simply perplexed me.

"David...believe! Believe! Believe!" Samantha shouted over and over as she held my hands tighter and tighter. "Say it now...'I believe!'"

"Ummm...okay...I believe," I said...feeling pressured to respond.

"No! Say it like you mean it!" she shouted.

"Holy crap...what the hell is going on here?" I shouted in my head. Time stood still as feelings of awkwardness, embarrassment, and anger flooded my heart.

This wasn't exactly a normal part of our church services back home. First of all, we don't sit on a stage like we're more important than everyone else. We don't get all crazy rocking back and forth. And, we definitely don't start yelling at people when we pray for them!

What was she *thinking?*

In the meantime, I noticed that Samantha's nose was running from all her craziness, and she started coughing. Holding her hand to her mouth, she coughed violently and phlegm came out into her fingers. It was hanging down from her hand six or eight inches, and I started to grab a tissue to help her when she suddenly stopped me.

"No, don't wipe it away!" she barked. "Receive it as a gift from God!" She went ahead and wiped the mucous mess all over my hands as she continued to pray for me.

When I wouldn't respond in the way she wanted me to, she finally started yelling, "Come out! Come out of him now! Come out!"

This mother of four who was normally cute and kind had turned into a whacky, woman preacher doing voodoo on me with snot-medicine in the middle of India. At this point, I was *done* with this tele-evangelist circus. I looked Louis in the eyes and whispered, "This chick is nuts!

On the count of three, I'm ducking outta here...1...2...3."

I scooted in between two praying team members and ducked off stage. I was confused and frustrated with all the madness! I wasn't quite sure what was going on with her, but I didn't exactly appreciate this kind of attention.

Debriefing the Craziness

After the service was over, our team of six loaded back on the bus and started our journey to meet the other teams at an "old aged home" in Tippalakatta. Although I would normally be excited to see Pastor Prakash who runs the facility, my mind was spinning to make sense of what had happened with Samantha and prepare for a debriefing session that I knew would be required.

I was the first one off the bus, and I headed straight to find Michael and the other three leaders on the trip. We ducked behind one of the buildings, and their eyes grew bigger and bigger as I quickly shared about the entire ordeal. It was obvious that we needed to sort everything out and repair the team dynamic in the process.

It was decided that Dan Stone, one of our team leaders, and I would debrief the experience with Samantha while everyone else enjoyed another curry dinner. What I thought would be a 30-minute conversation turned into a three-hour debrief including a detailed rehashing of events and an accompanying theological and psychological dialogue about the source of all the craziness. While the rest of the team ate curry and gave away bags of concrete to villagers, we were huddled behind a building with ants swirling around us and kids peaking around the corner.

I shared about the experience from my perspective…how inappropriate her actions were in that setting and the natural embarrassment of it all.

"Samantha, if you are genuinely sensing that God is wanting to do something within my life, feel free to have a conversation with me. But, under no circumstances are you to start yelling 'come out!' and 'believe!' at the top of your lungs in front of over 100 people in the middle of frickin' India…"

"Well…was this something that God was telling me to do…or was it something demonic that came over me?" she was confused.

As we dialogued about the entire experience in depth, she began to weep once again. This time it didn't include the rocking back and forth or the incessant prayers that produced sweat. This time it was filled with embarrassment and awkwardness.

She looked up at me with tears streaming down her face and said, "David, I'm so sorry. I wouldn't want to do anything that would hurt you. I love you. I'm so sorry."

My heart melted with compassion.

As the other team leader stepped away to check on whether the team was ready to leave, Samantha and I continued to discuss the experience. We went round and round as she tried to understand where it all came from.

"I think you developed a great deal of compassion for me as we talked on the train ride," I explained. "I think you want me to believe in myself and what God can do through me, and you wanted me to respond in a certain way. When I wasn't responding quickly, you started thinking that this was your chance to see some demonic action in India."

I continued on by telling her that I wasn't sensing any sort of profound experience in the moment…with God or Satan. I just wanted her to stop making such a scene and to quit yelling at me in front of the congregation and the rest of the team.

She continued to cry and asked for my grace. I expressed forgiveness, and we talked about all of the great things that were still coming up in the second week of the trip.

As we boarded the bus to drive back to Suresh Kumar's home where we were staying, I sat in the right-hand front seat next to the window, and I motioned for Samantha to sit next to me.

With a bus full of team members behind us, it felt like we were all alone. As she was still upset over the experience, I put my arm around her, and she gripped my other arm tightly. We leaned into each other and talked closely the entire ride, and something began to intermingle in our hearts. What had been a painful encounter turned into a shared experience that I have never shared with anyone else...nor do I want to ever again.

The conversation that began on the train ride from Chennai to Tenali was now continuing along the dirt roads in the middle of India's rural villages. With the headlights of the van bouncing around in the palm trees...

I
was
in
heaven.

I was the middle school kid who always wanted to hang out with the pretty girl, but never had the courage to talk to her. I was the kid who would stand against the wall at dances and never peel myself away. I was the kid who kept my head down and wouldn't speak up in fear of embarrassment. Now, I was sitting beside a beautiful woman who needed *me* to comfort her...and I was glad to do so.

The Moon Looks More Beautiful In India

Each morning, we'd get up early and lather on our mosquito repellent as we headed upstairs to the third floor of Suresh's home. A curry breakfast was followed by a team devotional of singing and Bible reading. Then, we'd jump into the van and bounce along to a faraway destination that usually included a medical camp, water well dedication, orphanage, and an evening outreach meeting.

On an "off" night when we didn't have an event in a rural village, we'd hang out and enjoy relaxing with the team...which would periodically include a scooter ride for me. A day or so after the church fiasco, I borrowed a staff member's Bajaj scooter...sort of like a Vespa in the US, but a lot more dusty and beat up. I walked by the second floor living room and motioned for Samantha to follow me.

She made her way down the stairs behind me, and I stepped onto the scooter.

"Jump on. Let's go for a ride!" I said.

"No way! I'm not getting on that thing without a helmet...at night...on *that* road!" she resisted.

"C'mon. It'll be fun! Get on."

She relented and jumped on the back. With her arms wrapped around my waist, we pulled out into the busy, nighttime traffic and headed toward the open road. The faster I went, the more tense she became. With the wind in our hair, we headed down a beautiful, smooth road with the silhouette of the trees creating an incredible scene.

As I turned around to head back, I remembered what looked to be a lake or water reservoir...and a perfect place to look at the moon. We pulled off the side of the road and gazed at the moon shimmering on the Indian water.

As I looked over at her bright, shiny eyes, I commented, "The moon looks more beautiful in India, doesn't it?"

It was clear that a heart connection had developed as we debriefed that whole scene at the church. I had this tingly sensation whenever I was around her, and I wanted to feel it even more.

After we both admired the scene, I asked if I could give her a hug. She nodded her head, and we slowly embraced. As our bodies pressed against each other, my heart was pounding harder and harder with nervousness and adrenaline. It was about ready to leap out of my chest.

We got back on the scooter, and she wrapped her arms tightly around me and buried her head in my back. She pulled me close, and I felt a rush of emotion.

"Samantha, I really enjoy being with you. I want you to know that.

You're an amazing person," I said over the rustle of the wind. "Put your hand right here and feel my heart."

She released her grip and felt the beating within my chest. "That's what you're doing to me," I told her.

She drew even closer and said, "I love spending time with you, too."

That ride back to Suresh's house couldn't have lasted long enough. As Samantha scurried back upstairs, I asked our 70-something-year-old team member if she wanted a ride...as to seem that I was an "equal opportunity ride giver." Believe me when I tell you that having that senior citizen hold me close wasn't quite as fun. In fact, I think my heart almost gave out on that trip down the road and back.

Trying to Stay Focused

After revealing my feelings and sharing a warm embrace, my mind was now spinning with a desire to be with Samantha even more. Something had been unleashed within me that was dying to get out.

Throughout the next day, I would gaze at her as she wore a brightly colored punjabi...not exactly slimming to the figure, but I didn't care. I just wanted to be near her.

Samantha had both passion and compassion. She could manage the lives of her four children and look beautiful in the process. She was a fiery woman who didn't like to play it safe. She liked adventure, and she wanted to be increasingly involved in ministry.

I couldn't help but compare her to my wife who was thousands of miles away...and Laura was continually coming up short. Any remnant of connection with her was fading, and my obligation to our marriage was weakening by the moment.

For the first time in all my travels to India, I *wasn't* anxious to call back home. I finally had the capability to video-chat with my wife and two kids, but I really wasn't interested at all. I called once or twice, but I didn't want to see their faces or hear their voices any more. I didn't want to feel the deadness of my heart toward all that "home" represented.

As we continued to minister to people in need, I watched Samantha closely. We played with the orphans at the children's home, and I noticed her interactions with them. As we dedicated water wells, I was drawn to her love for the people in the villages. And...I also noticed that she was watching *me*.

There was a definite connection between us.

We found ourselves talking at each stop and sitting next to each other on the van. Our eyes would meet, and we'd smile at one another. Unfortunately, someone else was watching as well. That evening Samantha pulled me aside.

"David, someone noticed that we've been hanging out. We've gotta cool it," she warned.

"What are you talking about? Who said something?" I asked.

"Dan Stone...he noticed us and asked me what was going on," she responded. "I told him not to worry about it."

"Okay...not a problem."

I acted like it was no big deal, but I *hated* Dan for standing in our way. From then on, Samantha practically ignored me from sun up to sun down, but I kept walking up behind her and secretly whispering, "You look amaaaazing." She rarely initiated a conversation, and she steered clear of me for the most part. My heart was *dying* inside. I wanted to be close to her. I wanted to laugh together and share about all that was going on. Instead, I started to feel like I got dumped after going out with a girl for two days in middle school.

From time to time, Samantha *would* let me into her world, which included a much-beloved rickshaw ride from Suresh's house to a nearby water well dedication. As another teammate and Samantha hopped in, I squeezed my 6'5" frame inside the back of the motorized, bright yellow vehicle. We bounced around the road, and I rubbed her back as she tried to ignore her enjoyment. She'd smile at me and continue her conversation with the other gal. I was just glad I finally had an opportunity to connect with her...even if it was only for a few minutes.

Unfortunately, when it was time to head home, she didn't jump in the vehicle with me. Even though I understood, I was crushed. The truth is that she was protecting me...and us.

Later that evening, she pulled me aside for another chat on the porch. With her Bible and journal in hand, we sat down in the white plastic chairs.

"David, I love being with you, but we've got to stop. I don't want someone to notice us and cause a problem for you...or for me," she stated with force.

"Nooooo!" I playfully gestured. "I don't want it to stop!" I was being overly dramatic in a kidding sort of way to try to hide the fact that this was how I truly felt.

"Seriously. I love spending time with you, but both of us have our own families. After we leave India, we can't keep this up. You know that," she reminded me.

"I know...you're right," I quietly agreed. "Done. We're done...It was fun, but we're done."

Yet, I wasn't done.
She wasn't done.
We weren't done...and I was miserable.

Ironically, my friend Kirk Parker just *happened* to be visiting India at the same time. Although he was travelling separately, his trip coincidentally overlapped with ours. (Kirk was the guy who gave me my first shot at full-time ministry when he hired me as the Associate Pastor at ROCK-harbor back in 1998.)

I secretly wondered if God specifically sent Kirk to be with me during this time of temptation and weakness, because of his similar experience. After ROCKharbor exploded with growth, Kirk went through his own time of burnout and depression…and eventual moral failure.

If anyone could understand my feelings at a time like this, it would be Kirk.

One afternoon, I pulled him aside to share what was going on…not quite everything…just the part that wouldn't get me fired if it leaked out.

"Bro, I'm dyyying," I admitted. "I'm so burned out, and I just want to quit. I'm sick of ministry, and I'm sick of my marriage. Something has to change."

As always, he listened and compassionately communicated that he understood where I was coming from. After we chatted for 30 minutes or so, we agreed to re-connect back in the US and find a way for me to get some help. I was thankful he was there, and I knew God sent him to India…just for me.

A Train Ride Filled With Laughter
As our time in Tenali came to a close, we packed up and walked down the road to the train station. I stopped at one of the vendor stands to grab a cool drink for the ride, and I couldn't resist buying Samantha something as well. As we started to board the train, I unzipped the bag strapped on her back and slipped in the Sprite.

She noticed…and smiled.
Just what I was looking for.

Some Indian trains have sleeper cars with padded bench seats facing each other in small compartments so that six people can sleep in the same area…three bench seats directly on top of each other on the right and 3 on the left. I found my seat, and Samantha just happened to be sitting in the same compartment. David and five girls...this was going to be quite a giggle-filled, eight hour train ride.

The game of choice was "Slapjack." The loudest gal of the bunch dealt the same number of cards facedown to all of us, and the goal was to end up with the entire deck in your possession...in *my* possession I should say. Each player takes the top card on his or her pile and places it, face up, in the middle of the table. When the card placed in the middle of the table is a Jack, you slap your hand down on it to win the entire pile of cards. Loud, raucous, and a lot of red hands from all the slapping.

Samantha and I were both competitive to say the least. I slowly placed my leg up against hers to create tension and distract her from winning. The more my pile began to increase and hers decreased, the madder she became. Her nostrils flared with intensity, but I just kept smiling right at her. She was obviously resisting the connection, and I thought it was all quite amusing.

Willing to Risk it All
After arriving at our hotel in Chennai, the leaders on the trip went about the arduous task of getting our room keys and assigning roommates. Although this is done in advance, there are always issues that arise. In this case, there was an extra room, because there were an odd number of team members.

"David, we'd like to give you your own room since you're the pastor...a little extra space for you," Dan Stone generously offered.

"Okay...that's fine," I agreed.

I realized *exactly* what was happening. I was being given an opportunity...wondering if this was a test from God or a temptation from Satan. Frankly, I didn't care. As I stepped onto the elevator alone, Samantha walked right in behind me. I couldn't believe all this was coming together.

"Hey…I have my own room. I'd really like you to stop by and join me," I invited. "Let's just watch some TV together and relax…nothing more."

With a slight smile on her face, she said, "I'll think about it…I'll call you in a minute."

My heart was racing with anticipation. I was nervous, excited, and hopeful. After changing clothes and freshening up a bit, I got all my stuff organized in the room…and I waited. It felt like an eternity, but she *finally* called.

"Hello?" I quickly picked up the phone. "Are you coming over?"

"Well, why don't you meet me down in the restaurant?" she asked.

"No, come over to my room, and let's just hang."

"I can't. It's just too risky. I don't want something bad to happen to you. I don't want someone to see us."

After a few minutes of persuasion, I finally relented and met her in the restaurant downstairs. She was already there when I arrived, and I scooted into the booth right next to her. We chatted awhile and laughed about the events of the trip. Then…her face settled into a seriousness that I hadn't seen since our last "talk" on Suresh's porch.

"Do you know what you're doing?"

"What do you mean?" I was dodging the subject.

"You know full well what I mean," she said in a direct tone. "Are you really ready to risk everything to be with me?"

"*Absolutely!* I don't care. I know that inviting you up to my room is like risking everything….but…I'm sitting here with you right now… ready to throw away my marriage…and my ministry. I just don't care any more."

She looked down at the table, and she didn't know what to think. I looked into her beautiful eyes and said, "I'm gonna go up to my room right now, and I'd love for you to join me. I'll be waiting."

As I left the booth and headed toward the elevator, I knew I was taking a risk. It's not as though I was planning to have sex with her that night...or even kiss her. Believe me when I say that I didn't have sex before marriage, and I was pretty much a rule follower up until this point. I played by the book as much as I could, because I didn't ever want to disappoint anyone...especially my parents since I played the role of a "good boy" my entire life. I was willing to risk everything in this moment...just to spend a few moments with her alone.

I walked into my room, turned on the TV, and laid on the bed...and I waited...and waited...and waited. After 30 minutes, I kept trying to convince myself that she still might come. After an hour, I started to cry. I knew that I was in a desperate place if I was willing to throw away a 15-year marriage and 10 years of full-time ministry to simply hold Samantha close to me and watch TV on the other side of the globe.

What had my life come to?

I cried myself to sleep that night as I listened to Jack Johnson sing to me on my iPod. When I woke up the next morning, my pain and desperation had not disappeared in my dreams like I had hoped. Things were just as bad, if not worse.

Before heading out on a shopping expedition at the local Chennai megamall, it was our custom to hold a three-hour debriefing session to talk about all the amazing things that happened on the trip. As the pastor of the church, it was my role to lead this meeting.

In my soul-parched state, I had no idea how I was going to lead this meeting with any sense of integrity. Not only was I overwhelmed by the task in my present condition, but I had to face Samantha once again. She stood me up the night before, and I wasn't looking forward to seeing her face.

The truth is that I was dying inside, and I had no one to talk to. My mind was racing...trying to figure out what to do. Then, I remembered Kirk. Kirk was eight hours away back at Suresh's house. He was the only person I could imagine calling at that moment.

I hurried down the hallway and borrowed a cell phone, and I placed the call. Kirk was awakened, and I immediately started spilling my guts.

"Kirk, I didn't tell you everything," I confessed. "Not only am I miserable in ministry and in my marriage, but I've started to connect with another woman."

He listened intently as I poured out my heart with tears streaming down my face. I paced back and forth in the marble-floored hotel room, and I spoke of how my life was a wreck. I explained that I didn't want to live like this anymore...punctuated by a few pain-filled f-bombs.

When I stood up every Sunday morning to preach, I was focused on teaching something that I was genuinely seeking to live out in my own life. There was no way I could live my life without integrating all that I was learning and teaching. Otherwise, I would lack integrity. My insides wouldn't be matching my outsides.

For the first time in ministry, I knew *that* had happened. My deep longing for a life partner and affection was creating such a deep fracture in my heart and life that I was willing to walk away from everything. I was not okay with this. I knew I needed help, and I knew that I needed to take a break from the 70-80 hours a week I had been working for five years straight.

Kirk did his best to piece me back together over the phone before I prepared for the debrief meeting.

As everyone filed into the chilly meeting room on the bottom floor of the hotel, I could feel the impending need to share my life. I started our time together by having everyone check in about the trip. When it came around to me...the last one to go, I knew I had to be honest...but not *too* honest.

"Guys, I gotta tell you…I'm in a dark place," I shared as my emotions began to well up. "This trip has been tough for me, because I feel so dry inside. I'm really struggling. While all of you are experiencing so many great things because of what I'm producing…I'm dying. I have to take some time off when we get back home."

Tears were streaming down my cheeks as people got up from their seats and surrounded me. One by one they began to pray for me. Hands placed on my shoulders and arms as a symbol of togetherness. I continued to weep and cry as even Samantha prayed for my spiritual and physical health.

I sensed a cathartic release as I felt the love and support of the team.

A Tour Turns Into Indian Love

As everyone else loaded into a bus and headed toward the mall to pick up gifts for loved ones, Samantha and I were scheduled to continue exploring the city for an orphanage location. Would she stay or would she go?

To my surprise, she jumped right in, and I was even more attracted than ever to her compassion for those in need and her spirit of adventure. While the translator navigated from the middle seat, Samantha and I sat in the back. We gave input on where we wanted to go and kept our eyes open for the perfect spot.

"How are you doing?" she asked.

"I'm okay. I'm glad you joined me."

"Why wouldn't I?"

"I don't know…I just thought…well…I thought you wouldn't want to be around me anymore," I admitted.

"Not at all...I'm *excited* about finding a home for the kids today."

"You gotta know that everything I shared this morning...well...it doesn't change the way I feel about you." As I bared my soul, Samantha stared straight ahead. She eventually looked over and simply smiled.

With each stop to take a look, the level of awkwardness dissipated until it was completely gone. As she slid over to sit close to me, I reached down and touched her exposed calf. I slid my hand up and down to massage her weary legs from two weeks of constant walking. She reached over and took hold of my hand as we smiled at one another. The excitement of touching her body was exactly what I had been wanting all week long.

I started anticipating our time in the car more than our time looking at potential buildings. With each car ride to the next location, our level of interaction increased. As we leaned back in the seat with our heads turned face to face, we placed the palms of our hands together on her lap. As our fingers playfully laid on top of each other, there was a moment when our hands almost clasped together as a couple naturally would.

She hesitated...I hesitated...and, then it happened.

It was a simple threshold that we had not yet crossed. Our fingers interlocked, and it was a step of intimacy that would be nothing to the average couple...but to two people in our position, it was foreplay that was both ecstatic and electrifying. The intimacy that came along with holding her hand caused a rush of emotion and adrenaline that was all encompassing of my body and soul.

I wondered if our translator, a Harvest India pastor, noticed the fact that we were staring into each other's eyes and holding hands in the back seat. Frankly, I didn't care, and it made it even more exciting to know there was a chance that we'd be caught. I was finally with her, and it was as if we were completely alone.

Instead of sharing a cigarette in the post-orgasmic moment, we did the safe Christian thing. I passed her one of my earbuds, and I dialed in a playful song that I knew she'd get a kick out of...

You're a part time lover and a full time friend
The monkey on you're back is the latest trend
I don't see what anyone can see, in anyone else
But you

I kiss you on the brain in the shadow of a train
I kiss you all starry eyed, my body's swinging from side to side
I don't see what anyone can see, in anyone else
But you

Here is the church and here is the steeple
We sure are cute for two ugly people
I don't see what anyone can see, in anyone else
But you [2]

We didn't find a place for the orphanage that day, but I found a place in my heart for Samantha. I was falling in love, and I didn't see anyone else but her.

Our Plane Ride Home

We re-joined the team, and I knew our interactions would need to stop. As we walked into the Chennai airport, I didn't want to leave India without giving her a gift. I didn't know what was going to happen when we got back home, but I didn't want her to forget about our time together.

Having already purchased a gift for my wife, I was now on a new mission as I entered the gift shop and looked for a piece of jewelry that would suit Samantha's taste and passionate energy. I searched high and low as other team member's shopped in the tiny space. I was nervous that someone would notice me buying something that may not end up on my wife's neck later on.

I found the perfect item...a deep red, beaded necklace with a beautiful, sterling silver clasp...handcrafted in Chennai. I knew she would love it. I had the gentleman place it in a special red velvet-lined, black box. I

walked toward our team as they were lined up to check in their bags, and
I noticed Samantha in the back of the line. I casually came from behind
and slipped the package in her carry-on bag.

"Don't open it until you're onboard," I whispered. "I think you'll love
it."

As we scattered to our seats, I didn't see her on that first leg of our three-
flight journey home until we finally landed in Kuala Lumpur, Malaysia
for a half-day layover. While most of the team members took a long nap,
a few of us opted for a tour of the city…including Samantha. Although
I had been on the tour before, I enjoyed checking out the tallest towers
in the city once again, and we eventually made our way to the butterfly
garden…one of my favorite spots.

"Samantha, you've got to check out the back of the garden where the
monkeys play on top of the tall nets," I encouraged. "C'mon, let's go see
what they're up to."

As we made our way to the back of the garden, I knew this was my one
shot to have a serious conversation with her on the way home. I knew
I could blow everything with one question…but I was willing to ask it
anyway.

We looked up and saw the monkeys playing about. Now was my chance.

"Samantha, would you like to try and make this work back home?" I
boldly asked.

After a long hesitation, she responded, "I can't…I just can't walk away
from 15 years of marriage and my family. I'm sorry…I just can't."

My heart sank. It was like I had finally peeled myself away from the side
of the wall at the middle school gym and asked for that coveted dance.
She said no, and I walked in the opposite direction. I didn't even know
what to do. I moped my way back to the tour van, and I just sat there. I
was sad, broken, and felt stuck.

"What do I do with all these emotions? What do I do with all this pain?" I asked myself.

I didn't want to stay in Malaysia, and I definitely didn't want to face my life back at home. In fact, I emailed my wife and told her that I already had a ride home from the airport.

"You and the kids won't need to pick me up," I wrote.

I knew this would send a signal to her that would be awkward and disconcerting at the same time. Frankly, I just didn't want to face them. I wanted to curl up in a little ball and hope the world would just go away. Unlike most flights, our entire team was separated in the seating arrangement; hardly any of us were seated together. As I sat toward the front of the plane, my heart was sinking. I wanted to be with Samantha…just to sit and talk, but I didn't think it was possible. I was sitting all alone listening to music when I pulled out a notebook and started to write.

"Samantha, I miss you already. You are more beautiful than the moon shimmering over the Indian waters. Your eyes shine brightly into my soul, and I love you. I want to be with you, but I understand that it's not possible. Please don't forget our time together. Love, David"

I folded the paper up and headed back a few aisles toward her seat where she was sitting alone in a row of three. I planned to just hand her the paper and keep walking, but she invited me to sit down. She read the note, and we began to talk about the last two weeks.

Within a matter of minutes, it was clear that she had experienced a change of heart. She nestled her head into my shoulder and looked up at me with her glimmering eyes. With 14 hours of flight time, we literally spent hours upon hours talking about life. From our favorite foods to our dreams for the future, we covered every topic we could possibly think of…until we fell asleep snuggling up next to each other. From time to time, I'd wake up and look around to make sure we weren't being watched. We'd listen to some music together and continue talking.

I'd lean over and kiss her on the cheek and whisper in her ear, "You're amaaaazing, and I...love...you."

As the pilot announced that we were an hour from LAX, Samantha said, "David, I need to be alone now. I have to face my husband and kids when I walk off that plane, and I need to be ready for that."

"I understand...it's over. Right now...all of this is over," I said. "I have to go back home and figure out what life is going to be like for me. I'm going to take a sabbatical from leading Revolution, and I've got to figure out the whole marriage thing, too."

As I turned to look her in the eyes a final time, I said, "You're amazing... and I love you...don't forget that."

I stood up from the seat, and I made my way back up a few aisles. I sat down, and I turned on some music that soothed my soul as we made our descent.

Our team headed toward baggage claim, and I could feel the heaviness of my steps toward the home that I wasn't being drawn to. I could feel pain swirling in my head and heart. I didn't want to see Laura or my kids, and I just wanted Samantha to go away. I wanted to forget all of what had happened. I asked a team member for a ride home, and I just wanted to leave.

Between the woman I didn't want - and the woman I couldn't have - I would have liked them both to disappear.

As I made my way through immigration and headed up the ramp toward the exit, I was enjoying the last fleeting moments of quietness when I caught a glimpse of my family out of the corner of my eye. My kids were wearing broad smiles and holding big signs saying, "Welcome home, Dad!"...and they were there to greet me.

"*Shit*...why did she come here?"

I tried to disguise my displeasure, but it shook me to the core.

I did my best to muster up a hug and kiss for everyone, but my wife knew something was wrong. She knew that I wasn't the same person who left two weeks prior.

As we crossed the street to head to the car, I said, "Laura…when we get home…we need to talk."

SHOULD I STAY OR SHOULD I GO?

chapter three

The ride home was cold and icy even though it was a mild, southern California evening of 60 or so degrees. As soon as we got in the van, the kids popped on their headphones to watch a DVD, and I just stared straight ahead to avoid any eye contact with my wife. The kids were clueless as to the tornado of emotions that were swirling inside the vehicle or of the words that would be strewn about after they went to bed.

Anger was brewing as I thought of how I was going to say all of this to Laura. I wasn't necessarily mad at her, but I was angry about the entire situation. I was completely frustrated with how stuck I felt in our marriage and ministry, and I was exasperated that I couldn't just fly off into the sunset with Samantha and forget about everything else. I didn't want to have to articulate what I was mustering up the courage to say.

I was scared to death. I was scared of her reaction, and more than anything, I was scared of the consequences. I always like to know the probable outcome before I make a decision, and I had no clue as to what was about ready to transpire. As my heart pounded with nervousness, I sat silently...praying that she wouldn't ask a single question. The 25-mile trek home seemed like it would never end.

Each time I take a long trip, I bring the kids something back that we can't get here in the US...perhaps to assuage my guilt of being away from home for so long. As soon as we pulled onto our street, Waverly and Emerson started begging to rip into my suitcase to pull out their gifts from India.

I was weighed down by loads of guilt about my role in our home. I knew that I wasn't carrying my weight, but I didn't know how to change...or maybe I didn't really want to. I hated the thought of Laura working and doing all the housework and taking care of the kids while I constantly focused on ministry. Greater guilt came over working most Saturdays finalizing my message prep and every single Sunday at church and leadership meetings that took up the entire day.

The worst guilt of all came in knowing that I didn't even really enjoy spending time with my kids. They drove me nuts with their incessant questions and emotional highs and lows and constant needs. And, they were a consistent reminder of my own selfishness and my desire to be the center of attention. Hanging out with my family didn't exactly amass the accolades that my ego yearned for.

Thank God for gifts from India that alleviate the guilt...at least for a day or so. After the packages were ripped open and teeth were brushed, Laura began the bedtime routine. With each passing second, it felt as though an impending time bomb was ticking down to its final moments. As soon as their heads laid down, Laura walked straight into the bedroom where I was unpacking my suitcase.

"So, what's up?" she asked.

"I'm *done*," I said bluntly.

She just sat there and stared at me.

"I'm *done*," I said again. "I'm *done* with our marriage, and I'm *done* with ministry. I'm sick of living this way. I hate it, and I can't handle it anymore."

Once again, she just sat there, and then the words I dreaded the most came out of her mouth.

"Do you want our marriage to be over?" she asked with intensity in her eyes.

My eyes darted away to avoid the emotional weight that came with the question.

I said, "I'm not saying that I want our marriage to end. I'm just saying that I'm done with how it is right now. I'm not okay living this way anymore."

That was completely true. I wasn't sure I wanted our marriage to end, but I did know that I needed a lot of help to sort everything out in my heart. And, I knew I needed some time off from the frantic pace I had been running.

We went to bed that night in silence…no kiss, no hug…just silence.

Starting to Fidget
On Monday morning, I got up and waited awhile to call my boss, Rob

Mason. Because of his hard-driving persona and take-no-prisoners mo-
dus operandi, I was more than nervous about calling him. Would he start
whining about me being a wuss? Would he tell me to suck it up? Would
he deny my ability to take some time off? All those things were running
through my head.

"Hey Rob," I started. "When I was in India…I um…uh…I realized how
burned out I am…and uh…I could really…uh…need some time off…
um…"

He was surprised…not *that* surprised…but definitely caught off guard.
He didn't realize I was in that bad of a spot, and I didn't even tell him
how bad it really was. Seriously…who wants to tell the head of your
denomination, "Hey, I'm really burned out, and I'd like to be with this
other woman besides my wife, but I can't…so I'm feeling really depressed…"?

Not so much.

"Wow, I didn't realize you were that tired. I knew you were feeling it
a little bit, but I didn't know," he responded. "Well, let's start with 30
days, and see how you feel after that. I don't want to push you, but after
a month, I'll have to do something about Revolution. We can't just leave
it hanging out there."

"Great. I gotta get my head straight in 30 days," I was thinking to myself.

I called an "urgent" meeting of my Lead Team to share the news.

The Lead Team consisted of my key staff members who helped hold the
vision of the church and make important decisions. Rather than having
a board like many churches, we opted early on for a church led by those
doing day to day ministry versus a bunch of business guys sitting around
talking about service times and carpet color.

I rehearsed my need for time off and delivered it with a few less "ums"
than with Rob, but I don't think my team was very surprised either.

They could see it coming. I had been telling them for months that I was burning out and that I wanted out, and Michael (our Downey campus pastor who was on the India trip) already heard me voice the idea for a sabbatical during that final debriefing meeting. They were quite supportive, and we spent our time making plans as to who would take on what roles. Rather than have someone deliver the news for me, I chose to film a short video that would be shown at all 3 locations during the Sunday services.

During that same meeting, we gave my friend Kirk a quick call to get any insights from him and receive his support. They asked Kirk about his suggestion for a timeline of my return, and he indicated that we shouldn't put a definite time to it. "Just let things play out," he said.

"Kirk, I'm *really* going to need to hear from you when David is ready to come back," Jessica said with intensity. "I don't trust him to tell us when he is healthy enough to return."

Not surprising. I'm not sure she ever trusted me.

This was all very typical for Jessica...a hard-nosed woman in her early 30s that acted like she was 50-something...and dressed like it, too. I hired her as an associate pastor to raise up leaders to help people connect and grow spiritually at our church. A few people took to her, but most people couldn't handle her anaconda instinct. I loved her ability to organize and get things done, but she squeezed the life out of most people... including me. Unfortunately, my inability to lead her with confidence was definitely a great source of stress in my life to say the least.

As I drove home that day, I could feel the weight of the world lifting from my shoulders. All the heaviness of the financial decisions, the staffing issues including Jessica, the sermon prep, and everything else that goes along with leading a church with three locations was gone. Okay, it wasn't *really* gone. All those issues were still there, but I got a "break" from all the worries and stress.

Ironically, within an hour or two of getting home, I was fidgeting with anxiety.

Key leader conversations – check.
Suitcase unpacked – check.
Bed made – check.
Dishes done – check.

Now what?

I was already starting to feel the withdrawals from the frantic pace that I had been running for years. I didn't know what to do. I didn't know where to go. What would my time be filled with? After an hour or so of reading and praying, I was ready to *accomplish* something…yet there was nothing to accomplish.

Then, I remembered…I *did* need to call my therapist.

As I was pacing hurriedly back and forth in that hotel room in India pouring my heart out to Kirk, I knew that I needed to get help from several people when I got home. A therapist named Randy Powell was one of them.

I first went to see Randy when I was a 19-year-old student at Southern California College. I believe I was suffering from some sort issue with a female, and I sought out the free counseling services on campus. He was the perm-haired, big-smiling, director of counseling at the time, and he was extremely helpful through the process. When Laura and I got engaged during my junior year, we started going to pre-marital counseling with him, and he officiated part of our wedding with my dad.

Randy is an energetic therapist with a deep love for people, and even though we hadn't spent hardly any time together in 15 years, I knew that he believed in me. I also knew that he would be a safe place to turn to since he had a legal obligation to keep his lips sealed tight. He also seemed to have the power to help people change more than any other person I knew…and boy did I need some of that in my life! So, I called to make an appointment. At $150 an hour, I was motivated to experience some change.

She Calls

As I continued to fidget my way around the house, I heard my phone vibrating. I had asked people not to call me, because I didn't want to be tempted to jump into "work" mode.

It was her. Not my wife...but Samantha.
It had only been 24 hours since I saw her.

Before I could even pick up the phone, my mind was flooded with questions...first of which was, "Why the hell is she calling me?" We made it very clear to one another that everything was over the moment we walked off that plane. We weren't planning to re-connect...but my heart was aching to talk to her.

"Hey..."

"How are you doing?" she asked.

The sound of her voice sent a warmth through my body that was both soothing and disconcerting all at the same time. It was comforting to hear her care for me, but I was unnerved by the initiation of her phone call on our first day back.

"I'm okay. How about you?" I asked.

"Fine...just worried about you, and I wanted to check in on you."

I shared about my experience of calling my boss and meeting with the Lead Team, and she listened intently to all the craziness that was going on in my head. She listened to me worrying about the direction of the church, the finances, and what on earth I was going to do for the next 30 days.

When I get overwhelmed, I process verbally. There's something about me that requires a verbalization of all that is going on within me in order to sort it out. I have to hear it come out of my mouth before I can realize what's going on inside my heart. Talking to myself never seems to work, but talking to Samantha was amazing.

She listened attentively, and I felt like she deeply cared. She didn't just listen out of obligation or with a blank look on her face. She took in every word as if it was a hidden gift, and she re-packaged it for me to understand more deeply.

I was shocked that she called, but so glad she did.

"I miss you."
"I miss you, too," she echoed.

Her voice settled down my heart and mind. I wished that things could be different. I wished that we could somehow be together, but I knew that it was impossible. I wanted to see her again, but I knew I shouldn't suggest it.

Instead, I turned my energy toward writing. I wrote a short book in the previous year, but I had never written any songs. Creativity was begging to get out of me, so I put pen to paper. Within a day, I had scribbled out some semblance of a folksy song, but I needed some help putting a tune together. I'm not really musical at all, but I just needed to accomplish something...even if it was writing a little ditty that cleared out what was going on inside my heart.

I gave a quick call to one of our worship leaders at Revolution, and he agreed to stop by and come up with something together. He had no clue what I was singing about, but he was more than willing to put a tune to it...

> *Broken promises*
> *So many in my life*
> *Between me, myself, and I*
> *I've got broken, broken promises.*
> *Like brittle records, icicles, and a windshield in a crash*

Broke into little pieces
I've got broken, broken promises.

I was starting to feel like there were so many broken pieces in my life that they couldn't be put back together. Frankly, there wasn't enough glue in the entire world.

The Road of Therapy Begins

On Tuesday, I walked into Randy's counseling office at Vanguard University and sat down on the couch. I reached over and grabbed one of the drab-colored pillows piled in the corner specifically placed there for people like me...people that need to grip something tightly as those deep-down thoughts and emotions start welling up.

"So, what's going on?" he asked.

I proceeded to catch him up to speed on the last 15 years of life, and most of my time was spent going on and on about languishing in my marriage and in ministry. After confirming the legal confidentiality of our conversation, I spilled my guts about Samantha.

"Randy, she's amazing. I'd *love* to be with her, but I don't think that's possible. She isn't open to it, and the relationship ended when we walked off the plane," I said. "Except...she called me yesterday."

He never talked about Samantha or asked anything else about her. His focus was on my marriage and me. He asked about the rhythms of our life and my work and the possibilities of transformation.

"David, do you think God has the power to transform your marriage? Do you think he can restore it to the type of relationship that you're longing for?"

"Yeah...of course...God is God." I knew all this in a heady theoretical sort of way. "He can do whatever He wants, but I don't want to do the work He'll require in order for that to happen."

I felt like I was in a pit…a deep, dark hole that seemed impossible to scale.

"I'm in a 15 year-long rut that's a mile deep, and I don't want to climb out. I'd rather blow the whole thing up and just start over."

I could tell by the look on his face that I was in trouble. And, you know you're in big trouble when your therapist wants to meet with you two days later. Not that I'm in trouble with him or with God or anyone else… I could just tell that I was in deep water and sinking fast.

My homework was to take time to sit with God…by myself…with no books or music…just sit and take in His love. In my head, that was a sure way to fidget to death, but I agreed to give it a try.

Working It Out
I knew I didn't want the life I had been living, and I was ready to start making some changes…beginning with my physical health.

I hated the way my body looked, and I hadn't used my gym membership in months.

When we got married, I was 21 years old and weighed 175 pounds at 6'5" tall. I played sports my entire life, and I stayed active during college with body boarding and pick-up basketball games here and there. Then, I got a desk job.

When I got hired at that paper distribution company right out of college, I spent 3 months getting trained on the road. They gave us $25 a day to spend on food, and I spent it all on drive-thru lunches and steak dinners. Meanwhile I was sitting behind a desk all day taking orders for every known paper on the planet. I learned a lot about paper, and I also started packing on the pounds.

By the time I went to India in 2008, I weighed 215 pounds, and I felt miserable. Even though we live a couple of miles from the beach, I never wanted to go to, because all my flabbiness would be exposed. I know, I know. 6'5" and 215 pounds is no big deal. Frankly, most people still saw me as skinny, but I wasn't used to all that extra cushion around the torso.

With the extra time on my hands, I got to the gym immediately. I jumped on the elliptical machine and popped in my headphones. With every step on the machine, I'd envision myself running after Samantha and away from all the pain. I'd feel the anger deep down inside and push even harder and faster. For a guy who wasn't used to sweating much anymore, every bead that formed on my forehead and plunged down my face felt like an expulsion of my old way of life.

I was working it out of myself. I wanted the flab off my body and all those negative feelings out of my head and heart. I wanted to look better...for myself...and for Samantha.

Until that point, I ate fast food at least once a day...if not twice. I grew up eating all that fried goodness, and I loved it. There was something comforting about rolling through a drive-thru and munching on those fries as we cruised down the road. I re-lived that comfort day after day as I soothed myself from all the worries of ministry.

After coming home from India, I quit fast food...cold turkey.
I knew that stuff was killing me.

I started eating breakfast for the first time in 15 years...yogurt and granola. I began to eat a healthy lunch and fruits and vegetables for snacks. It felt good to make a change, and it felt even better to see the pounds start to fall off.

Coping with the Chaos
That first week back from India was truly chaotic. I was fidgeting feverishly...trying to find something to do with my time. I was working out once or twice a day, and I was eating differently for the first time in my life. Yet, my head was just spinning with all the possibilities.

Should I go back to leading Revolution, or should I just quit? Am I going to stay with Laura or move out? What am I supposed to do with my life?

All questions swirling in my brain.

When Laura and the kids would get home from school, I was at home, but I wasn't *really* at home. My mind was wandering aimlessly through the chaos. It was if I had stepped into a foggy jungle that I knew was inside of me, but I had never dared to trespass. I was finally exploring recesses of my heart and head that I had never been willing to investigate. I started to think about the *real* reasons why I was doing things in my life…questioning my commitment to everything.

You see, I grew up in a family where your "yes" meant "yes" and your "no" meant "no."

When I first started playing sports, I remember a particular season was rather difficult, and I wanted to quit. I wanted to walk away, because I wasn't that great at it yet. I knew other kids at school quit stuff from time to time, but in my family, we never quit.

"Son, when you commit to doing something, you carry it through. You never back out and you don't quit," my Dad explained. "That's just how it is."

So, I never quit. In fact, I swung the opposite direction, and I excelled in most everything I tackled. I wanted to prove that I was exceptional… even trying to be the best. If you gave me something to handle, I'd take such great responsibility for it that you'd never even question it again. I cared so deeply and passionately about everything that I was known as the guy you could truly count on.

But, in *this* moment, all I wanted to do was quit. I didn't care about the value of commitment anymore. I had been committed to everything my entire life, and I was done being committed.

Not anymore…I was *done* caring.

At one point, I explained to my therapist, "My 'care bucket' is empty. I've been caring about stuff my whole life that I'm completely out of care. I just don't care about anything anymore."

I didn't care about my marriage, and I didn't care about ministry. More than anything, I didn't care about what anyone else thought. I was sick of caring about other people's opinions, and I was done with all that.

Within days of returning home, I wrote in my journal...

> *My heart is so heavy with grief and pain. I don't care what's right or wrong. I just want connection. I want to feel loved and cared for. I want my heart to pound. I want to experience the adrenaline rush of excitement that comes along with a new relationship. I want out. I want out of the boredom, pain, and worry. I want out of a dry situation. I'm willing to sacrifice it all for joy, peace, comfort, love, and affection. I don't care what the cost is.*

The one thing I did care about was Samantha...especially when she called a second time.

I was shocked that she called again, but I was also ecstatic. All I could think about all day long was her. I wanted to hear her calming voice, and I wanted to be with her more than anyone else.

"Whatcha doin'?"

"Just doin' some laundry...and thinkin' about you," she responded.

"Hmmm...I miss you...when can I see you?" I knew this was pushing things, but I just couldn't resist.

"I can't see you...not now...maybe sometime soon though," she answered. She left the door open, and that's all I needed...something to hold on to.

All I wanted to do was see her, and all she wanted to do was talk on the phone. We'd call each other multiple times a day, and talk for up to an hour at a time. I say "talking" but there was quite a bit of just hanging out. It was that lingering that you'd do in high school or college…at night…when you didn't want to tell the other person good bye. We'd just sit there…hearing each other breathe…waiting for the other person to say something that would make us feel warm and cozy inside.

After a few days, I was done with that as well. I wanted to see her. She was afraid of someone else seeing us, but more than anything, she was afraid that seeing me would ignite something inside of her that she just couldn't stop. She joked on several occasions that if we ever kissed, it would all be over for her at that moment. So, hanging out on the phone was a way to get close…but not *too* close. By Wednesday, I finally couldn't take it anymore. I jumped in my car and headed toward her house, and I called her on the way.

"Hey…I'm around the corner." I was ready to be a little playful to see if she'd respond.

"No you're not!" she protested.

"Oh, yes I aaaaam…see you in a minute."

She was walking out the door to pick her kids up from school, but just the sight of her made my heart leap for joy. She opened the front door and nervously bounded down the front concrete steps toward my car. I rolled down the passenger window as she sheepishly looked around her cul-de-sac to see if any of her neighbors were watching.

I reached out my hand and held hers…only for a moment. The warmth and softness of her hand sent a rush of adrenaline through my body that hadn't been felt sense those moments we cuddled on the plane. For that moment, I was completely at peace and felt her care.

She jumped in her SUV, and we drove our separate ways…fueled by the momentary touch.

Seeing Samantha provided a relief from the pent-up desires to be in her presence. Now I wanted to see her even more. Later that day I suggested that we meet up for a walk on the beach. Once again, she said that she'd think about it.

I couldn't tell anyone about the chaos going on inside me except for my therapist Randy...and Kirk, my friend who had walked through a similar experience seven years back. I started calling Kirk at least once a day as soon as we got back from India. I'd pour out my heart on the phone to him again and again.

"Dude, I don't know what I'm going to do. I can't see myself continuing on like this. I just can't do it," I said...over and over...in any number of different ways.

Kirk has a knack for listening and not jumping in with his own opinion that much. He has this belief that God is powerful and will guide each person and that jumping in with "unsolicited advice" just doesn't work out that well.

In reality, when I ask for advice, I'm not really asking for it so much as wanting you to re-affirm what I believe is true. So, when I ask you for advice and then you don't give me the right answer...I'm usually bummed at you. The nice thing was that Kirk doesn't really give advice that much. He just listened...a lot.

The Email To End It All
By Thursday, I was finally starting to get in the groove of my new life... at least as much as four days could allow me to. That is, until I got an email from Samantha. Our multiple calls a day came to a screeching halt with the arrival of an email that ended it all.

Dear David,

I enjoyed our time together in India so much, and I'm so fascinated by you. Your care for me and willingness to listen to me make me feel so good inside, but I know that I'm a distraction for you and this new journey that you're on. We must stop communicating and return back to the friendship that we once had. I'm praying for your family and your marriage.

Please understand.
Samantha

"Crap! Why did she have to do that?"

I didn't *actually* think that things could continue as they were going, but she didn't have to end it via email. *What the hell!?!* Who ends a relationship via email? You've got some serious issues if you're not willing to face the person that you're with and just click "send" on an email.

I was fuming mad, frustrated, and overwhelmed. The one thing that was soothing my soul during all this turmoil and chaos was now gone. I headed to the gym, and I worked out harder than ever. The pounding of my feet on the treadmill and the gushing of sweat from my pores felt like an expulsion of all the disappointment within me...at least for an hour or so.

This email provided great fodder for discussion at my second therapy appointment for the week. Randy and I started wrestling with my motives for ministry and more importantly life. The more we talked about ministry and marriage...the more frustrated I became with my situation. I didn't know what to do, but I definitely wanted out.

I felt like a caged animal that had walked into the enclosure on its own accord. I willingly stepped inside of set of values and assumptions that I was now finding cumbersome (at best) and lethal (at worst).

I was still in such a fog that I had no idea how to even find my way out. When my family got home at night, I retreated to the comfort of an Internet connection and did my best to remain withdrawn from much of any interaction.

Within a few days of my return from India, Laura was dying inside, and she made a call to a counselor for herself. She was starting to lose weight as well...not from working out, but from a lack of sleep and a lack of eating. I hated to see her going through this, but I didn't want to tell her anything.

After the kids went to bed that evening, she asked, "So, how did counseling go today?"

"Fine...we're just working on some stuff," I responded.

"Is this about Samantha? Somebody told me that something happened with you guys in India. Is this about her?" she interrogated.

"No! It has nothing to do with that. I'm just wrestling with stuff," I nervously answered.

She let my ambiguous answer go, and she kept doing the laundry. I sat down in front of the television, and I'm not sure we had another exchange that evening. Each night was filled with the deafening sound of silence. I didn't want to talk, and she didn't know what to say.

During the middle of the day on Friday, my cell phone rang, and I saw that it was Samantha again. I let it ring and ring, but I finally picked it up.

"Are you trying to *kill* me?"

"What do you mean?" she asked like a little girl.

"What do I *mean*? I *mean* you that you keep calling me and wanting to hang out on the phone, but you don't want to see me in person. Then you email me to break things off, and now you're calling again. What the *heck?*"

"I just miss you...I don't want to stop talking to you. I'm sorry," she apologized in a soft voice.

"I love you Samantha...do you *realize* that?" I was trying to get this through her thick skull.

"Yes…I love you, too."

After a few more calls on Friday, I suggested that we meet up for an early morning walk on the beach the next day. She finally agreed.

A Text Message Changes Everything

On Friday night, I crawled in to bed with the anticipation of receiving an awakening text message. When I got home from India, I stopped charging my phone in the kitchen. Instead, I plugged it in on my side of the bed closest to the wall so that there would be no chance of a missed call or text message that might be seen.

I mentally prepared my exit strategy with clothes, shoes, and briefcase for some early morning "reading" at Starbucks. If the text message actually came, I'd grab my things and slip out the front door before my family even woke up.

I went to sleep…wondering if she'd stand me up again like that night in India.

At 6:07am, I was awakened to the beautiful sound of a vibrating cell phone on the carpet under my side of the bed. I carefully turned over and read five amazing words…"Meet you in fifteen minutes?"

I was finally going to be with her. Adrenaline shot through my body and my palms began to perspire. I couldn't wait to see her.

I jumped in the shower, brushed my teeth, and quickly slipped on my shorts, t-shirt, running jacket, and shoes. I grabbed my briefcase and scurried out the door without anyone noticing.

I called her on the way, and we planned our rendezvous location behind a set of businesses down the street from my house. She was already there when I pulled up. I parked my car, and I jumped in her husband's black Dodge Charger.

She leaned over and gave me a warm hug, and I was giddy with excitement to see her once again.

"Where do you wanna go?" she asked.

"Let's go for a walk on the beach."

"No, that's too dangerous." Her eyes opened wide. "I think someone may see us there."

Her nervousness quickly rubbed off on me, and I reclined my seat so I wouldn't be seen as we headed down the road. My hand clasped hers on the gear shifter, and I was in *heaven*.

At 6:30 in the morning, the one place we were absolutely sure that no one would see us was on top of Signal Hill, a hilltop park surrounded by a nice neighborhood that overlooks Long Beach. The closer we got to our destination…the more I raised my seat up.

I didn't know what was going to happen once we got to the park, but I was simply excited to be with her. I hadn't see her in six days, and I just wanted to be near her and hear her voice without the use of a phone.

She parked the car, and we walked side by side up the walkway on this chilly February morning until we reached a bench that overlooked the city. I hesitated to hold her hand, because I didn't want anyone to see us. I sat down on the concrete bench, and she immediately cozied up to me in my lap.

The warmth of her body on top of mine was better than any warmth I had felt in ages. She wrapped her arms around me, and placed her cheek against mine as we looked through the foggy sky down onto the city below.

"It's so amazing to be with you," I said. "Can you feel my heart?"

"Yes, it's about ready to pound through your chest!" she realized as she placed her hand on me.

Her eyes began to close as she leaned in toward my lips. She softly placed her mouth on mine, and she began to passionately kiss me. The moistness of her lips against my mouth created an energy that I didn't know if I'd ever feel again. The rush of excitement of kissing another woman other than my wife was amazing…the first time in over 16 years.

After a deep, warm embrace, she dropped her head and exhaled, "I knew I should never have kissed you."

"Why?" I asked softly.

"Because I knew that I'd love it," she said and leaned in to kiss me once again.

"I never planned on kissing you today," I admitted. "You're the one who said you didn't want to…"

"That's because I'm afraid of what it will do," she interrupted.

Despite our best efforts to keep warm by cuddling and kissing, we were both developing quite a chill in the coolness of the morning. Once again, we walked side-by-side back to her car. After turning on the heat, we continued to kiss passionately, and I slowly lifted her shirt and rubbed the soft skin of her side and stomach…wanting even more of her.

Neither one of us wanted it to end.

It was already getting close to 9am, and we both knew that we had to go home eventually. As she reached over to hold my hand on my lap, I reclined my seat, and she drove me back to my car. She was right… something had changed, and I would *never* be the same.

What Do I Long For?

The next morning, my family got dressed for church, but I headed to Long Beach Christian Fellowship instead. With my announcement being shown at all three locations, I wanted to avoid anyone at Revolution and try to clear my head through some music at another church.

I connected with the pastor of this church, Doug Richardson, when we moved into Long Beach back in 2003, and he had been very gracious toward me. There was something about him that seemed rooted and long-term. He had been in the city quite some time, and he was well-regarded for his character and ministry.

As I walked into the sanctuary of the church, I felt the reality of what it's like to attend a church for the first time. I was nervous and hoping no one would recognize me.

On this particular morning, I was surprised to hear that he was speaking on the subject of "intimacy"…quite ironic considering that's what I was longing for. I knew deep down that this message was for me.

"True intimacy is about nearness, and false intimacy is about numbness. False intimacy is about coping, and true intimacy is about communing," Doug shared. "When nearness isn't an option, numbness seems like a great alternative."

"Yes, I want nearness…I don't want numbness," I said to myself. "I've been living with numbness for years."

"Don't you long to have your heart entwined with another that goes beyond romance?" he asked from the pulpit. "Nothing can replace passion!"

"Yes, that's *me*," I said in my heart. "That's what I want."

"There are some of you here today that have things pressing down on you that are supposed to be under your authority, but you have let them take authority over you. This is a pivotal moment," he warned.

As the music was coming to an end, I scooted down the aisle to avoid seeing anyone familiar. I walked out to my car, and my mind was filled with thoughts of intimacy on the drive home.

That's exactly what I was longing for…true intimacy.

Doug hit me square between the eyes that morning. I started to realize that I wasn't just looking for sex or romance or freedom. I wanted intimacy with another person. I wanted to know and be known. I wanted someone to share my hopes and dreams with. I wanted someone to laugh and cry alongside. I wanted a true intimacy that was experienced with someone that you're willing to walk through the fire of life with.

I wanted intimacy with Samantha.

Getting Serious About the Future
Monday finally rolled around, and I could talk with Samantha more freely now that Laura and the kids were back at school. With each passing day, our conversations grew more intense with discussions about the future.

"Samantha, I really want to be with you…and I'm not just talking about today." My words were filled with passion. "I'm talking about *forever*."

The other end of the line was quiet…silence even….and then, finally, she spoke.

"I want to be with you, too," she said softly. "But…I'm scared."

"What are you scared of?"

"I'm scared of walking away from 15 years of marriage with no conflict to be with a guy who has crazy dreams for the future."

"I get it. I get it." She acted as if I wasn't in the same position.

"I'm not sure you *do* get it," she interrupted. "Being with Ben has no risk. He never rocks the boat, and being with you would be a bit different to say the least."

She was right. Being with me would be crazy. Seriously…who walks away from a 15-year marriage with four kids to be with…their pastor?

Yet, that's exactly what we kept talking about.

On Tuesday, we met at the beach for the specific purpose of questioning one another about the future and what the possibilities might be like. I stopped by Target on the way to pick up a blanket, and I met her in a remote area of Seal Beach so as not to be seen.

After laying out the blanket on the sand, we cuddled up next to each other. With each rendezvous, our physical connection increased. From a hug on the scooter to clasped hands in the back of the car to a kiss in the park…until now…when she rolled over and climbed on top of me.

As the weight of her small frame pushed down on my chest, she stared me in the eyes, and I could feel her warm breath on my lips. As I wrapped my arms tightly around her body trying to pull her even closer, she kissed me again and again.

Knowing that her head was filled with questions of the future, I rolled her off of me, and laid on my side. I stared intently at her face as she closed her eyes.

"So…Samantha…what do you want to know about our future?" I asked.

Once again…silence.

She finally opened her eyes and responded, "What does the future look like if I choose to be with *Dave Trotter?*"

"It looks *great!*" I exclaimed in order to break the tension of the moment.

For the next hour, we went on to discuss my job situation, our kids, where we would live, and the repercussions on Revolution Church. And, we talked about what God thought about the whole thing.

"I'm not sure what God thinks," I said. "I doubt that he's really excited about this, but I want to be with you."

"Yeah, I want to be with you, too."

"Honestly, I don't really care. I'm done caring. I want to have a great marriage, and I want to be with you," I passionately shared. "I love you."

I didn't want to talk her into being with me. This had to be a decision that she made on her own, but I wanted to be clear about my level of commitment.

"Samantha, you've got to know this," I prepped her. "If we do this, the crap will hit the fan. People will hate us, and we'll lose all our friends. I'll have to get a job, and you might have to as well. But, you've got to know…I'm willing to walk through the fire to be with you."

"I know…I'm just not sure I can say that to you right now," she shared. "I'm still thinking about it."

"I get that, but I can't keep Laura in limbo for much longer," I said. "She has no clue what's going on, and she's dying. I've got to make a move sooner than later."

Frankly, I didn't think that she'd ever be willing to do it. That's why I was shocked when I got her call the next day.

"I think I'm about ready," she said.

"Ready for *what*?"

"Ready to move forward…" she responded. "To be with *you!*"

"Wow…okay…that's great…I…uh…" I stumbled through my words. "Well, let's talk about some sort of plan then."

I'm a planner by nature. I like to develop a plan and execute it, but this was starting to feel a little unwieldy. After four counseling sessions, multiple conversations with Kirk, and evasiveness with my wife, I was *now* plotting my exit strategy.

We could possibly tell our spouses on Friday evening.
We'll drive to San Diego for the weekend to avoid the shrapnel.
We'll return on Sunday and figure out the rest of our lives.

That wasn't much of a plan, but that's the best I could do under the circumstances. I called my friend Kirk to share the news.

"Dude...I think she might *actually* do it."

"Do *what?*" he asked.

"I think she's *actually* going to leave her husband to be with me." It was as if I was trying to talk myself into accepting it. "Can you believe that? I'm *shocked.*"

I think Kirk was shocked, too. He was quiet for a bit, and then in an uncharacteristic moment, he got direct. Kirk is usually filled with compassion, and he uses a very indirect manner to convey his opinions...rarely stepping across the "I'm-gonna-give-you-advice" line. It wasn't like he was trying to correct me like a dad...it was more like a big brother who was warning me of the impending pain.

"Dave...you know what you're about to do, right?" he asked. "I can't stop you, but you do know that you're about ready to destroy life as you know it. Do you realize that?"

"Yeah...I get it." I didn't really have a clue. "I'm willing to do it for her. I'm ready to make this happen."

Before everything could happen, I had to get through one last orthodontist appointment on Wednesday afternoon...with Samantha's husband.

The Timeline Moves Up
I was planning to get my braces off and be fitted for a retainer, but things didn't quite go that smoothly.

"Dave, it looks like you'll need one more appointment to get these things off," Ben said in his usual friendly manner. "I want to make one last tweak before we fit you with a permanent retainer."

As always, he wanted to take extra special care of me as...his pastor.

"Dang it! The likelihood of another appointment is slim and none after you find out that your wife is leaving you for me. I'll never get these things off now!" I yelled in my head.

Yet, I casually responded with, "No problem...I can wait."

As I mentioned, I was sweating with nervousness that he was on to us, and I didn't really want to have a fistfight in a dental office with a bunch of middle schoolers cheering their orthodontist on to crush the face of a local pastor. In fact, I *did* know that he was on to something.

Earlier that week, he walked in on Samantha texting, and she told him that it was me. A day later, he heard her on the phone with me and asked, "How's your *boyfriend* doing?"

Not good to be called a "boyfriend" by the guy who puts sharp objects in your mouth. Luckily, I got out of the parking lot without a fist to the face or a dental tool shoved up my nose.

The next afternoon, Samantha and I planned to meet at South Coast Plaza for a little shopping and dinner. I had a counseling appointment that afternoon, and I told Laura that I didn't want to fight the traffic home. I'd just grab a quick bite and be home a little later. I didn't think that she'd be all that bummed since I was completely checked out every evening anyway.

As Samantha and I strolled through Nordstrom looking for a pair of over-priced jeans for her, I became increasingly nervous by the minute. What if someone saw us? What would we say? What if Laura calls right now?

We made it through the mall and settled on a secluded restaurant for dinner. We talked through our impending decision, but I still thought that she'd back out. I didn't think she had the guts to actually do it.

As we sat in my car giving each other goodnight kisses, she whispered in my ear, "I wanna tell Ben tonight."

"Tell him what?" I couldn't believe what I was hearing.

"Tell him that I'm in love with you and that you and I are going to be together from now on."

"Are you *serious*?" I didn't like the sound of this plan. "Let's wait until Friday so that we can do it at the same time and then get out of town together."

"No, I want to do it *tonight!*" She was very clear about her choice. When Samantha is sure about something, I knew that I needed to step aside. I was nervous about the outcome and absolutely shocked at her willingness. I thought about leaving Laura on numerous occasions, but I never actually planned to do it for one reason.

It wasn't the kids.
It wasn't the sanctity of marriage.
It wasn't my commitment to her.
It was ministry.

If I wasn't married to Laura, I knew that I'd have to walk away from being a pastor. I was *so* in love with my role as a leader of a church that I stuck with my passionless marriage.

But not anymore. I was *done* with ministry, and I was *done* with my marriage. Samantha was ready to walk away from Ben, and I was ready to walk away from Laura. "Could this really be happening?" I asked myself as I drove back to my home.

It was almost 11pm, and I was praying that Laura was asleep already. It was past her bedtime, and I didn't want to have to deal with any questions. As I walked into the house, I immediately noticed that all the lights were out...except for the one on her bedside stand.

Her head was propped up with two pillows, and her arms were tightly grasping the covers on top of her. As I undressed, she weighed in, "Where have you been?"

"The mall," I responded without emotion.

"I don't deserve this!" she yelled. "I don't deserve to be treated this way. You come home from India and say that things are over, but you're just leaving me hanging out here. I can't sleep, and I'm losing weight. I don't deserve this!"

I didn't respond. I climbed into bed, and I just laid there. She turned out the light, and I hoped to God that it was over.

I could hear her start to cry...not the one-tear-at-a-time kind of cry... the sobbing kind...where you feel like there is something about ready to explode.

"ARE YOU HAVING AN AFFAIR?
JUST TELL ME IF YOU'RE HAVING AN AFFAIR!"
she yelled as tears dropped on the pillow.

My heart sunk.

I was mortified that our marriage had come to this.

I didn't know what to say.
I didn't know how to respond.
I rolled over...dead inside...and eventually fell asleep.

I SHOULD GO

chapter four

On Friday morning, I laid in bed until Laura and the kids were out the door on the way to school. I didn't want to feel the glare of her eyes or deal with the questions from the kids about what we were planning to do that evening. I just laid there anticipating the day ahead.

It was a *big* day...a monumental day in fact.

The question of whether I should stay or go had been answered. I doubt I would have ever left Laura on my own without someone else to go to, but I had Samantha. We had each other. We were making a united decision to leave our spouses to be with each other for the rest of our lives. We weren't exactly sure of all the details when it came to where we were going to live, how we were going to support ourselves, or what was going to happen in terms of our children, but we did know that we were going to be together. That's what *really* mattered.

I also knew that this was going to be a day like I had never experienced before in the 35 years of my life. Although there was some nervous anticipation, I was numb to the degree of my impending highs and lows for the upcoming day. I was a man on a mission…not unlike every other day of my life. Yet, this day's mission was like no other.

I hit re-dial to find out how last night went over at Samantha's house.

"Hey babe," she answered the phone.

"Helllloooo gorgeous," I said in a pseudo-Barry White tone. "How did last night go?"

"It was rough. He didn't get angry or anything. He just started crying and begging me to stay," she reported.

"Ouch! That had to have been tough," I felt for her. "What did you say to him?"

"I said, 'Ben, I'm in love with David, and I'm leaving you to be with him,'" she said with no emotion. "It wasn't really that tough. He just needs to get it in his head that we'll have to find a way to make this work."

"So, how are you feeling?" I dug a little deeper.

"I'm okay…I'm ready for today to be over and have a great time in San Diego with you!"

"Yeah, I'm looking forward to that, too," I said nervously. "I just have to get through today."

Preparing to Drop the Bomb
Getting to San Diego that evening seemed a million miles away considering all that I had to do in order to get there. It wasn't as simple as packing a bag and locking the door behind me. I needed to do the "right" thing and inform the people that mattered in my life…namely Laura.

My plan was to spend the day writing letters to Laura, my parents, Rob Mason, and an official resignation letter to the Lead Team.

This wasn't going to be something that was hidden or done secretly. I wasn't going to sneak away for a weekend rendezvous in San Diego and act like nothing ever happened. This was a radical change of course at the one-third point in my life. I knew that my choice was going to significantly impact the lives of hundreds of people, but I assumed that they'd get over it pretty quickly.

Seriously...how important am I? It's not like they can't move on with their lives and forget about me.

Rob will find another pastor to lead Revolution.
The church will keep doing its thing.
People will forget about me within a few months.
My parents will deal with it.
Laura and I will figure out how to parent together....apart.
And, my kids will get through it somehow.

It won't be that bad. At least, that's what I kept telling myself.

I opened up my laptop and started the first letter...to my parents. In weird way, I knew that this one was going to be the most difficult of all. Even though Rob had threatened to cut off my penis if I ever had an affair and even though my wife might be utterly devastated, I had this feeling that my parents may take it harder than anyone.

As an only child, I had been showered with attention from both of my parents my entire life. They showed it in different ways, but I knew that they both loved me tremendously. My Mom expressed her love by telling me how great I was and that she would always love me no matter what. My Dad said that I could have pooped on a plate as an art project and my Mom would have said, "I love it!" It's true. My Mom gushed over me constantly, and I virtually could do no wrong in her eyes.

I remember in 10th grade when I got caught cheating on a German test…I thought my Mom was going to be depressed the rest of her life. Her sweet, precious son who was an "A" student had now shattered her image of his perfection. She knew I wasn't perfect, but she liked to believe I was.

My Dad, on the other hand, knew I wasn't without fault. He liked to see himself as the counter-balance to my Mom's gushing. Not that he was hypercritical, but he definitely had high expectations for me…primarily in the area of grades. He pushed me to excel in large part because his parents didn't push him. They let him slide by when he could have excelled even more. I think he was trying to make up for it with me.

If I got a "B", I was pushed to get an "A." If I got an "A," I was jokingly asked if there was extra credit.

That kind of stuff takes a toll on you…at least it did for me.

During college when I started waking up to my own identity, we had it out about grades and the like. I started to push back, and that caused a father/son friction that we had never had before. I was always the kid who went along with everything pretty well.

I didn't drink.
I didn't smoke.
I didn't have sex.
I didn't even listen to secular music.
I was the good Christian kid that did what I was told.
I was responsible, and you could count on me.
But I was sick of that now, and I had to drop the bomb on my parents.

Hello Mom and Dad,

I never thought I'd write a letter like this, but it's the place that I have come to. I am choosing to share this information with you via text, because a voice-to-voice conversation would just be too painful.

First of all, let me say how thankful I am for all you have provided for me over the past 35 years. I cannot believe how you've invested in me, trusted me, and encouraged me. I am so thankful, and I believe there has been incredible fruit in the process.

Secondly, let me say how sorry I am. I have failed you tremendously. I have carried out all the external duties of life, but my internal world has suffered tremendously. I blame that on no one other than myself. Ironically, I have done the right, practical, and strategic thing my entire life. I live every day trying to figure out how to maximize every moment, and that is absolutely exhausting. Frankly, I'm finding that my drive is fueled by a tremendous amount of guilt that controls me.

I have cared about everything my entire life. Anything that is given to me is taken on with such great responsibility. Unfortunately, I've run out of care. My care box is empty. For a variety of reasons, I don't care about my marriage or ministry. That is so foreign to me, but it is liberating in a way – freedom from the crushing weight.

During my time in India, it became very apparent that I have been seriously miserable with ministry and marriage. Neither one are giving me what I want, and I quickly realized how willing I was to throw them both away as I began "connecting" with a member of the India Team. With an intense craving for connection, I was starving to be with someone who would care about me and want to connect on multiple levels.

I thought that taking some time off for a sabbatical would re-energize my "care" and help me get back on track. The result has been a greater degree of disenchantment with my marriage and ministry and an intensifying connection with this woman.

Although I was attracted to her a bit over the last 3 years, there has been no pursuit or inappropriate / extra contact. Before going to India, I found my mind wondering what it would be like to connect with her. Through some very weird circumstances, that connection happened. There was a connection that resulted in a tremendous amount of talking and heart sharing – no kissing and no sex just to clarify.

It spun me out, because it caused me to realize what I was lacking in my life and what I really wanted. Through a great deal of conversations, she has made it clear that she wants to be with me, and I want to be with her.

Please know that I'm not oblivious to how wrong this is, how many people I'll hurt, and the devastation that will result. I've been talking about it with my therapist and Kirk Parker for two full weeks. I am fully aware that I'm "blowing up" my life.

After making the right decisions my entire life – generally in order to gain the approval of others, I have made a decision to radically change the course of my life that will piss a lot of people off. I'm so bummed about that, but I'm committed to my decision.

Tonight, I informed Laura that I have been so disconnected from her for the past 10-15 years that I'm done. We are brother and sister more than anything else, and that is not working. I am seeking a divorce, and Samantha and I plan to move forward in life together. She informed her husband and extended family last night of our intentions as well. Beyond the obvious complication, Samantha is one of Laura's best friends and she is the wife of my orthodontist.

Frankly, I'm scared to even talk to you. I don't assume that you'll want to talk to me in any other voice except a raised one. I'm so sorry for disappointing you and hurting you in the process. I will be out of town on March 8th and 9th, but you are welcome to contact me after that via email. I've already starting looking for a job, and there are many new hopes and dreams for the future.

We'll see what happens.

Love,
David

After I typed my name at the bottom of the document, my eyes scanned to the top of the page. I began to re-read every word audibly to ensure that it said exactly what I wanted to say…leaving no room for misunderstanding. As got to the word "divorce," my lips began to quiver with emotion. My eyes started to well up with sadness knowing that I would be crushing my parent's view of their son as the successful pastor, loving husband, and doting dad.

I had failed them.

I had not lived up to their expectations, but I didn't want to try anymore. I didn't want to be that responsible person that did the "right" thing any longer. I wanted freedom, and I wanted intimacy.

I saved the document, and I started on the next one to Rob, my boss at the denomination. This one was hard in a different way. I hated to disappoint my parents, but I was actually *fearful* of Rob. He had invested so much in me, and I was a bit nervous that he might come after me. I put my head down and just banged it out…trying not to let the emotions slow me down. After I was done with his, I wrote the official resignation letter to the church that I assumed would be read in public…a Christian press release to satisfy the political requirements of the organization.

Dear Lead and Oversight Teams,

After two weeks on my sabbatical, it is with great regret that I write to inform you that I am no longer able to fulfill the role of Lead Pastor within Revolution Church. As the founding pastor of this wonderful community, I recognize the high calling of leading with passion, conviction, and integrity. At this point in time, I do not believe that I am able to fulfill these three qualities.

Over the past five years, I have given every ounce of my heart and soul to the planting of Revolution and the extension of the Kingdom of God. Unfortunately, I underestimated the cost to my family and my soul in the process.

Because of the condition of both, I believe that it is best for me to take a step in a new direction. This will give me the opportunity to continue re-engineering my life, and it will give Revolution the opportunity to continue on with a revolutionary vision.

Despite all my shortcomings and recent burnout, please know that I have faithfully taught God's Word and led our church family to the best of my ability through the empowerment of the Holy Spirit. Please trust that God has genuinely worked through me and within you during these precious years.

In Ephesians 3:14-21, Paul says…

"For this reason I kneel before the Father, from whom his whole family in heaven and on earth derives its name. I pray that out of his glorious riches he may strengthen you with power through his Spirit in your inner being, so that Christ may dwell in your hearts through faith. And I pray that you, being rooted and established in love, may have power, together with all the saints, to grasp how wide and long and high and deep is the love of Christ, and to know this love that surpasses knowledge - that you may be filled to the measure of all the fullness of God. Now to him who is able to do immeasurably more than all we ask or

imagine, according to his power that is at work within us, to him be glory in the church and in Christ Jesus throughout all generations, for ever and ever! Amen."

That is my prayer for myself and for Revolution Church as you continue as a movement of revolutionaries who follow Jesus, love our neighbors, and impact our world.

Igniting a Revolution,
David Trotter

Brutal.
Absolutely brutal.

Even though I was sick and tired of leading the church and dealing with the complainers, I had invested everything in this group of people. I gave every waking moment to the growth and development of Revolution Church. And now…I was walking away. I couldn't take it any more, and it grieved my heart that I couldn't figure out a way to make it work.

I was done.

After saving this document, I began my final letter…my letter to Laura. My plan was to clearly articulate everything I wanted to say and then read it to her in person that evening after the kids went to bed. I would read her the letter, send each letter via email, grab my bag, and pick up Samantha.

Word by word I slowly typed out everything that had been stewing inside of me. I told her that we were acting like roommates and that I was *done*. I told her that I was sorry and this just couldn't go on. And, I told her that it was Samantha. She was the one for me.

As I finished the last word and saved the document, I sat in our living room in silence…staring at my computer screen…numb to what I had just done.

"I finished," I exhaled as I called Samantha again.

"How does it feel?"

"Okay...a little numb I guess. I'm glad it's over," I admitted. "Now I just have to tell her."

"Yeah, that'll be rough, but I'm here for you. You can do it," she cheered me on.

Packing My Bags

Since I was only planning to be gone for the weekend, I didn't need to pack much. Just a few outfits for San Diego would suffice. I'd be home on Sunday evening, and I figured I'd start sleeping in the garage until Samantha and I could get a place of our own.

I grabbed some jeans, a couple of shirts, and pair of tennis shoes. I tossed my toiletries in a plastic bag, and I placed several pairs of socks and underwear in the side pocket. The sight of underwear triggered my anticipation of the evening.

Even though I was excited about our time together, I had not fully processed through our first night alone. I booked a nice room at the Double-Tree Hotel, and I started to envision what it would be like.

Would we walk in and tear each other's clothes off?
Would we stare awkwardly at each other's naked bodies?
Would we turn on the television and fall asleep to the late night news?

The reality is that I would see her naked for the first time, and she would see me. I assumed that we would make love, but I didn't want to force anything. Yet...how could we not? We were going to spend the rest of our lives together, and this night was the beginning.

"What if I don't meet up to her expectations?" I thought to myself.

"What if my penis is too small or my body is too fat or I accidentally let out a fart while we're making love?"

I felt like I was back in 7th grade as I prepared to kiss Becky Adams for the first time outside my junior high school at the Harvest Festival. My mind was now racing with every possible scenario that could go wrong...from getting excited too quickly to not getting excited enough. I was a wreck with anticipation and fright as I thought about our first night together.

I wanted to be fully prepared though. I didn't want to drop our bags, get passionate, and find her looking back at me with a blank stare because of my lack of preparation. So...after I packed my bag, I jumped in the car and headed down to the drug store.

I had never purchased condoms before, and I didn't even know where to look. I started at one end of the store and zigzagged my way back and forth looking for small boxes like the ones that Laura bought before she started taking the pill. Finally, on the next to last aisle, there they were... in a locked case.

"*Crap!* Now I have to ask someone for these things!" I screamed in my head.

After finding an effeminate, blue-vested clerk adorned with a gold chain and one shiny hoop earring, I hesitantly mumbled, "Um...I need some help in aisle two with the locked case." I was just praying that he knew what was in the locked case on aisle two so that I wouldn't have to explain it to him around the other shoppers.

He got the hint, opened the case, and retrieved my selection...a large pack of 24 ultra-ribbed condoms. I wanted to be *really* prepared.

As he scanned the item at the checkout, he raised his eyebrows and gave me a slight smile as if to say, "Go get 'em." I felt like my gay uncle (if I had one) just gave me a wink as I was walking out the door with my prom date. Yes, it was as awkward as you're imagining.

The Bomb Detonates Early

By mid-afternoon, I was ready for Friday to be over with. I was ready for Laura to put the kids to bed, and I was fully prepared to read her the letter. Unfortunately, someone got to her before I could.

"Hey," I answered my phone for the 20th call from Samantha that day. "David...she *knows*," she said with a sadness in her voice.

"She knows *what?*" I asked fearing the worst.

"Laura knows about *us*. Ben called her in the middle of the day and told her everything."

"What an *asshole!*" I yelled. "I can't believe he'd do that. Didn't you tell him not to? I wanted to be the one to tell her."

"Yeah, I told him last night, but he's just being a big *jerk!*"

"What the *hell* am I going to do *now?*"

"I don't know," she said. "But I've started getting calls from Jessica and other people at Revolution, and they're heading over here. They're coming over to try and stop me."

"Are you kidding me? He told them, too?" I blurted out. "Let me call Laura, and I'll be right over. Let's just get out of here."

"No, you can't come over," she warned. "They'll crucify you. Let me throw some stuff in a bag, and I'll meet you in 15 minutes. Just call her!"

I was already in the car, so I headed toward a local coffee shop that had free Internet access. The closest parking spot happened to be open, so I pulled right up near the front door. I opened my laptop, and I dialed Laura's number.

"Hello," she answered as if someone had died.

"Hey…I guess you've heard," I stuttered.

"Yep." That's all she said. I wasn't expecting so much silence. I figured she'd unleash a tongue-lashing on me.

"Well…I…um…was going to talk to you tonight after the kids went to bed, but I guess it's too late now….um…I wrote a letter to read to you," I stumbled. "Do you want me to read it to you now?"

"No," she said as if I was an idiot.

"Okay…well…I guess I'll just email it to you."

"I can't believe you're doing this. Is this really want you want to do? You really want to end everything this way?" she asked.

"Yeah…this is the decision I've made." I paused to take a deep breath. "I want to be with her."

That was it. It was over. She finally knew. Actually, I think she knew long before that moment, but I finally had the guts to confirm it. Unfortunately, she had to find out from someone else. To make it worse, it was Ben.

I clicked "send," and the dreadful email left my computer to mark the end of our marriage. I quickly sent emails to my parents, Rob, and our staff and Lead Team at Revolution. I breathed a sigh of relief, and I aimed my car toward our meeting location.

Samantha dodged multiple people who were waiting in front of her house and pulling up to the curb, and she called me on the way.

"I can't believe these psychos!" as she was screaming like one. "Do they really think that coming over to my house is going to stop me?"

The mere sight of her SUV pulling up behind my car on the side of the road brought relief to my mind. She was there, and she hadn't backed out. I hopped out of my car, locked the doors, and jumped in the driver's side of her vehicle. We turned off our cell phones, and we headed down the 405 toward our destination…leaving the past and the craziness behind us.

It was sheer madness!
My wife finding out early.
Ben rallying people to their house.
Samantha dodging them as she left.
People calling to try to stop us.

It was exhilarating to know that it was finally out in the open, and we could start our new life together. With each mile that passed, what we had done became more and more of a realization. We clasped each other's hands like the first time in the back of the car in India, and we smiled into each other's eyes.

We were *finally* together.

Our First Night Alone
As we walked up to the front desk of the hotel, we started to wonder whether someone may try to find us in San Diego and cause a ruckus. To ensure our anonymity, we explicitly asked that no one be told that we were checked in to the hotel. Although Laura could check the credit card records to see where we were, we had some sense of security in knowing that the hotel would not confirm our whereabouts.

We dropped off our bags in the room, and we found a nearby restaurant to enjoy dinner together. Our conversation was filled with recollections of connecting in India, the craziness of leaving that afternoon, and the concerned messages that were mounting in both of our voicemails.

We returned to the room, and I knew that this was going be a bit awkward. It was edging toward 9pm, and preparing for bed was imminent. As she took off her makeup and freshened up in the bathroom, I took the opportunity to pull out the box of condoms from my bag. I slid them in the drawer by the bed as to be ready at any point in time.

As she emerged from the bathroom in a cute set of pjs that she purchased just for the trip, I began to undress down to my ubiquitous white underwear. I tried to act as if I wasn't uncomfortable or nervous in disrobing in front of her for the first time, but how could it be avoided?

As she turned off all but one light, I slipped into bed, and she joined me. There we were...together...for the first time. I was finally laying in bed all alone with Samantha...a beautiful, sexy, adventurous woman who I was going to spend the rest of my life with. I was with the woman of my dreams.

All those years of longing for adventure and connection culminated in an unbelievably intense night of intimacy...and neither one of us were disappointed. Around 3:30 in the morning, we finally fell asleep in each other's arms.

Enjoying Our Weekend Together
The next morning we woke up, and the reality of what we had done was starting to sink in. It wasn't a feeling of regret, but it was a realization that the dream of waking up next to one another had actually come true. We were all alone in a hotel room snuggled up under the warm blankets, and we were loving it...no regrets.

After we both showered and dressed, we struck out on a day of exploring La Jolla, a quiet seaside community just north of San Diego. After a quick breakfast, we walked around the downtown area arm-in-arm. With no threat of seeing anyone we knew, we felt the freedom to be fully present with one another in public view. The freedom to simply be together was so liberating...holding hands, hugging, and kissing as two "newlyweds"...minus the wedding part.

As we walked from shop to shop, I continued to enjoy learning more about Samantha's taste in fashion and life. I found that she was a practical woman with a love for the simple things. She was fine dressing in jeans and flip-flops, but she did love her Coach handbags. I'm not sure how many she owned, but it was definitely her accessory of choice. And, on this day...she was also wearing the red, beaded necklace I purchased for her in India. Her short, blond hair was shining in the sun, and her large, dark sunglasses made her look like a movie star on holiday.

We found our way down to Casa Beach where seals are known to lay up on the sand. With a handful of protestors handing out literature about the endangering of the seals, we pressed through the crowds to get a closer look. After getting a glimpse of the cute creatures lying all over one another, we casually walked down the beach.

With my tennis shoes firmly laced up, I stepped onto the sand, and Samantha kicked off her sandals.

"Are you going to take those things off?" she asked.

"Nah, it's kinda cold...and I don't really like getting sand on my feet anyway," I heard myself explaining.

"Huh...if you're going to be with me, you're going to have to get used to the sand," she lectured. "I love the beach, and we're going to be here a lot!"

"Okay...I'm fine with that." I was willing to play along...a whole new thing for me.

"I'm serious. We're going to get you some flip-flops today!" She sounded like a flip-flop saleswoman trying to convince me on how great life with sandals really was.

As we sat there on the beach cuddling in the cool breeze, I started to get a glimpse of how my life was changing. We talked for hours about my excessive work schedule and how she did not approve. We discussed her love for adventure and my hesitancy to do new things. We went back and forth on her affection for spontaneity and my affinity with planning. On top of that, she made it very clear that there would be no television in our bedroom.

I had wanted adventure, and I was getting it. I just wasn't sure I wanted quite *this* much.

We got up from the sand, and we walked back up the stairs to the top of the cliffs that overlook the beach below. The unhurried stride of our walk combined with heartfelt conversation was slowing down the pace of my internal engine. All that horsepower that had been revved up for 10 plus years of ministry and the last two weeks of hiding my love for Samantha was finally starting to slow it down.

As we enjoyed a nice dinner on the water, we dreamed about our future together...raising kids, enjoying life, and growing old. We made love again that evening, and it was even better than the first night. We were learning how our bodies worked together, and our level of trust was increasing moment by moment.

Our First Sunday
The next morning, we woke up, and the dream was still a reality. We were lying in bed with one another, and we were having the time of our lives. Although voicemails from friends and family were filling our boxes, we ignored them for the most part. Samantha *did* call her sister to clear up accusations that I had somehow kidnapped her. She made it clear that she left on her own, and she was just fine. I, on the other hand, didn't call Laura or my parents back. Who needs to hear someone yell when you already know what they're going to say?

Instead, we were heading to church. That's right. It was Sunday, and it was our first opportunity to go to church together. After a little research, we chose to attend The Rock, a high-energy mega-church that has an incredible reputation in the San Diego area.

We swung through a McDonald's drive thru, and Samantha insisted that we both get Fruit'n Yogurt Parfaits, something I never would have ordered on my own. It was delicious, and I enjoyed the diversion from my usual sausage biscuit. This whole flexibility thing was starting to be fun.

After parking in the first-time visitor lot, we walked hand-in-hand through the barrage of patio tables where people were taking volunteer sign-ups. Entering into the auditorium, our eyes scanned the balcony for open seats. I was walking into church with Samantha for the first time, and I was anxious about what this was going to be like.

Was God going to strike us both dead?
Was I going to have to ward off an attack of guilt?
Was she going to wig out and start crying over her decision?

The music started, and I sensed a Divine Presence that was comforting to my soul. My antennae were up and ready to receive any of the negative experiences, but they never came. Instead, I sensed a Closeness that I hadn't felt in a long time.

As a familiar song was being sung that both of us loved, I reached over and held her hand. There we were on the second row of the lower balcony on the right hand side of The Rock Church...holding hands worshipping God together. I sensed a togetherness and partnership that I had never sensed before. The feeling of holding hands in church with the woman I loved was overwhelming. I didn't want it to end.

The pastor took the stage, and he began to speak on the role of the "ARMY" as they called it, those who were committed to following Jesus and being part of The Rock. That Sunday's topic was on "ministry and service"...in other words, volunteering at the church.

We happened to attend during the once a year "get off your butt and serve" sermon. I had given that message at least once a year, if not more often, over the course of starting Revolution Church. The degree to which pastors will twist the Bible about spiritual gifts in order to get you to pass out donuts on Sunday morning or take care of the snotty-nosed kids in Sunday School or drive the rickety bus to pick up loads of people who don't have their own car...is unbelievable. Whatever the motive...I wasn't buying it anymore. I sat there rolling my eyes, and I whispered the behind-the-scenes reasoning for the message to Samantha. It was all part of the business model of growing a mega-church that I had bought into...but not anymore.

The message finally ended, and I had to dig deep into the recesses of my brain to even remember the positive experience at the beginning of the service. We dodged all the pamphlet-laden volunteers who were trying to lure us into their booth to serve on their ministry team, and we made our way back to Samantha's SUV.

Samantha suggested a restaurant called Panera Bread, so we ventured down the street to their new location. Once again, the adventure of an unknown lunch setting combined with trying new food was part of the shift that I could feel over the course of the weekend. Something was happening within me. Expectations of life and the ordinariness of certain rhythms were disintegrating.

During lunch, we unpacked the message and then discussed our plans to head home. We were both anxious about seeing our spouses once again, and we wondered about their reaction. Her plan was to sleep on her living room couch, and my plan was to set up house in my garage. We'd eventually move in together once we got things figured out.

On our way home, we stopped by the outlet malls, and Samantha took me shopping for those flip-flops. After she bought me a pair of shorts and a shirt, she was on a mission to find the perfect pair of Rainbows – a brand of sandals that I just "had to have" in her words. We finally found a store that sold them, and I was ordered to take off my shoes and socks. I slid the tan-colored thongs in between my virgin toes, and they felt like someone was using a medieval torture device to get me to confess to a long-forgotten sin.

I was informed that they looked great on my ultra-white feet that rarely saw the light of day. As I walked back to the car in my new $50 sandals, I could feel the skin between my toes starting to cry out for mercy. Samantha loved them, and I was committed to making them work.

With each mile marker we passed as we drove home, I could feel the tension in my chest start to increase. I didn't want to surprise Laura by just driving up, so I decided to give her a call.

"I'm on my way home," I informed her.

"Well, you should know that you're *not* welcome." Her tone was tense.

"It's *my* house, too, and I don't plan on going anywhere," I said with conviction in my voice. "I need to be there for the kids, and *you* can't stop me."

"You're not staying with us," she demanded. "The locks have been changed, and you can find all of your stuff on the back driveway."

10 Plastic Bags

Laura was on her way back from Disneyland with the kids, and I was going to beat them to the house. When I arrived, I found out that what she said was true. All my clothes were shoved in black, plastic garbage bags on the back driveway. The locks were changed...all of them except for the door to our detached garage.

Since I planned to be living in there for a while, I started moving all my clothes into my new home away from home. When we originally moved in, we insulated and dry walled the ceiling and walls. Even though it was a little cool out there, I was well equipped to live for quite some time... a couch, refrigerator, and television were already in place. I was set to stay put in our family home in order to avoid any legal messiness over me being the one to leave. I did not want to be standing in divorce court with my wife saying that I was the one who left the kids. I was going to stay in that garage for as long as it took.

Soon enough, I heard voices on our front driveway, but I kept working in the garage. It was Dan Stone (the guy who was on to us in India) and a couple of other leaders at Revolution who Laura had obviously called to come over in her support. Eventually, my boss Rob Mason showed up as well. It was a party at the Trotter house, and I really didn't want any of them to be invited.

Laura finally showed up without the kids, and her face was filled with anger. After I provided a minimal greeting to her entourage, she motioned for us to sit down in the two chairs on the front porch.

She started in…"I can't believe you're doing this."

"I know…I'm sorry it has to end this way." My voice sounded rote with minimal empathy. I had been rehearsing my prepared responses.

"You're not just going to come back into our family home after traipsing down to San Diego and having an affair."

"They're my kids, too, and I'm not going to risk my custody by moving out of this house," I warned. "I'll just stay in the garage, and we'll work it out. Give me a key to our house."

"You're not going to stay in the garage!" Her voice was getting louder and quivering with anger.

"Fine. I'll be glad to call the police and have them come over here as I show them *my* name on the loan to this house," I fought back. "I can stay here if I want to."

"You *cheated* on me," she started to yell. "You cheated on me WITH. MY. BEST. FRIEND!"

As a flood of tears fell from her face to the concrete below, my head dropped in embarrassment as my leaders and boss watched me being yelled at by my wife of 14 years.

As she *finally* handed over a new key to the house, she begged, "Take half of our savings…$3,000…and this credit card and just go. I took my name off of it, and you can just use it….and here's the title to your car. Please just go! I don't want you here! You can't stay here! Please go!"

Her heart was breaking before my eyes. The trust of our marriage had been shattered, but she gathered as many pieces of herself together to take a stand.

I was disconnected...observing her brokenness like an outsider...unte-thered from emotion. I didn't know what to do.

My wife was yelling at me, and she had obviously received counsel from a number of people to just give me some money and instruct me to leave. I didn't want to risk the custody of my kids, but I also didn't want to cause greater pain by staying there.

"Fine...I'll check with an attorney over the next couple of days to see if this affects my custody," I relented as I held the new house key tightly in my hand. "If it does, I may choose to come back home and live in the garage."

"Please just go." I could hear her begging for a safe place to call her own.

I walked out of the front yard and down our long driveway that runs alongside our house. With my leaders and boss watching, I loaded 10 plastic bags of clothes, shoes, and belongings into the back of my Ford Focus. The humiliation was unbearable.

As I placed the final bag in my trunk and started to get in the car, Rob walked over to have a few words.

"David, just give her space," he encouraged in a soft voice. "Don't try to force anything on her. Just give her space."

"Well, I'll have to check with an attorney to see if it affects anything." I heard myself sounding so technical.

"Do you realize what you're doing right now?" He was being fatherly.

"Yep...I do." I wasn't interested in being the 'son' in this conversation. "Rob, you know that whatever I do, I go big. I don't mess around and do stuff half-assed. This is no different. I'm going all the way...and I want to make sure my rights are protected."

As I was getting ready to shut the car door, Dan Stone pipes up for the first time. He was the leader that helped me debrief the whole "cast-a-demon-out-of-the-pastor" experience with Samantha back in India. You have to know Dan to know that he's an exuberant 40-something with more energy and intensity than he knows what to do with…triathlons are one way that he tries to get it all out. And, he has *no problem* speaking his mind.

"Rights?" he yells. "You don't have any rights! You gave those up when you went to San Diego with Samantha!"

"Shut the hell up, Dan Stone!" I yelled back. "You don't know what the hell you're talking about! You're not in my shoes."

I got back in the car and slowly drove down Lemming Street…the street that Laura and I moved on to in 2003 with great vision for a new church. We passed out cookies to our neighbors to welcome ourselves to the street. We helped many of them choose to follow Jesus and become part of the church. Now, I was driving away devoid of the vision I came with.

By the time I made it around the corner, my heart was grieved with how I had responded in anger to Dan. I flipped a u-turn and headed back to my house. With the guys still standing on my driveway, I opened my car door and stood up.

"Dan, I'm sorry for how I just responded to you," I apologized. "I never should have yelled at you, and I wish I wouldn't have. Please forgive me."

He quickly countered with unrelenting intensity, "David, you don't have any rights…"

I was done with him. I turned to Rob with a condescending smirk on my face and said, "Rob…explain it to him."

As I laughed to myself, I drove away again. I rounded the corner and headed to a local shopping center to catch my breath.

Where was I going?
What was I going to do?

As I sat in my car with the engine still running, I picked up my phone and called the one person besides Samantha I could trust…Kirk Parker.

"I'm sitting in my car with a check for $3,000…and a credit card with a $32,000 limit…I guess this is how I start my life over…isn't it?"

48 DAYS OF HEAVEN (+ HELL)

chapter five

My next call was to Samantha to see how it was going as she tucked her kids into bed. We brainstormed my options, and the only one that made sense at 9pm on a Sunday night was a local motel. Rather than sleeping on her couch, she decided to join me for the evening.

As I drove down Lincoln Avenue, I started scanning both sides of the street for a good deal on a place to lay my head for the night. The first place I pulled into was the Peacock Motel. The one story structure was lit up by the neon glow of peacock feathers flashing to get the attention of people desperate for a place to stay...people like me.

The pleasant Indian man at the front counter slid open the glass window to inform me the rate was $65 a night for a queen bed...non-smoking. With $32,000 available on my newly acquired credit card, I wasn't *that* concerned about the amount. I handed him my driver's license and made some small talk.

"What part of India are you from?" I asked.

He mumbled some state...or city...that I couldn't even repeat if I tried.

"Ahhhh, I see," acting as if I was well informed. "I just got back from India two weeks ago. We were there on a humanitarian trip."

Somehow, I wanted to impress someone so they'd acknowledge that I was still a "good person" despite my waywardness in the moment.

He nodded and strained to even find a slight smile at our endeavor. I was waiting for the natural question of, "Why the hell are staying at my hotel when your driver's license says that you live around the corner?"

Thankfully, he didn't ask.

After texting Samantha the number of our room, I rummaged through a garbage bag in the back of my Ford Focus to find some clean socks and underwear, and I grabbed my bag of toiletries from our San Diego trip as well. Within a matter of moments, I heard a knock at the door. I pushed the drapes aside to ensure that my wife wasn't standing there with an ax in her hand, and then I opened the door to let Samantha in after I saw that it was her.

She tossed down her bag and pushed me onto the bed where she began to give me a stress-reducing kiss. After a few moments, we headed down the street to El Pollo Loco. I never seemed to make my way to that restaurant, but it appeared to be the only thing open. On her recommendation, I went for a chicken burrito, loco salad, and a Diet Coke…easy ice.

We ate in the room and debriefed our separate experiences of coming home to our spouses. Mine was angry, and hers was pleading for her to stay. I was surprised that *mine* didn't plead, and she was shocked that *hers* wasn't angry.

In fact, I was quite flabbergasted that my wife didn't even insinuate that she wanted me to stay. She didn't even hint at the fact that she loved me, cared about me, or wanted me back. All the more evidence that we were done.

Being the man of action that I am, I was ready to develop a plan. I wasn't going to be sleeping in a funky motel bed for a week while we tried to determine what to do with our lives.

"Okay, babe, we've gotta figure out what we're gonna to do tomorrow…" I started.

"Well…I'll leave around 6:30 and get the kids ready for school." You could see her beginning to process a new schedule in her head. "After I drop them off, I'll meet you back here, and we'll go from there."

"I'm thinking that the first thing we should do is find an apartment that will take a credit card. I'm not spending this $3,000 in cash until I absolutely have to."

"Why don't we just meet at the Starbucks by your house?" she suggested. "We'll start calling around for an apartment, and we'll call some attorneys, too."

"Attorneys?" I was confused.

"Yeah…I'm not waiting around for something to happen with his business. I want to know what's rightfully mine and get started on a divorce."

There was that word again. Divorce.

It sent chills through my body to think about looking for a divorce attorney...even more when I actually envisioned checking that box next to my name on a random questionnaire.

Monday, March 10th, 2008

The next morning, she woke me up with a kiss on my lips as she was headed out the door to get her kids ready for school. What a surreal feeling to kiss Samantha good-bye in the morning as I laid in a bed at the Peacock Motel as my own wife and kids were waking up just a mile away. My head was swirling, but I knew I could stabilize my mind by developing a plan action for the day.

I showered, checked out of the motel, and drove down the street to the Starbucks where we were to meet. Within a half hour, she walked in... freshly showered with a smile that lit up my heart. The mere sound of her voice saying, "Hey babe!" caused my heart to flutter in ways that it hadn't in years.

She pulled up a chair next to me, and we started searching through Google for an apartment. Should we get a one bedroom just for us? Or, should we even look for a house to rent that would work for all six kids?

That's right...*six kids*.

The guy who could barely handle putting his own two kids to bed by himself was now walking into a life where six kids would be the norm... her four and my two.

Although we had grand visions of a 4-bedroom house, my lack of income and the question of how much child support Samantha would be getting from Ben was telling us to get a one bedroom apartment.

The more we talked about our living situation...the more Samantha got fired up about what she wanted. At one point, it was as if a light bulb went on above her head.

"You know *what?* I'm not moving out of my house! *He* can move out and find an apartment on his own." This was the Samantha that I loved... and the one that scared me a little bit. "We'll get an apartment for you to live in for awhile, and I'll just go back and forth to help the kids. Within 6 months, you'll just move into *my* house with *me*."

I gotta tell you. I liked that idea. She didn't exactly live in a shabby house. Two stories of plush carpet, freshly painted rooms, a brand new kitchen, and new travertine tile that her husband had just laid in the downstairs entry....all on a beautiful cul-de-sac in the city of Cypress. I wouldn't mind snuggling up in her bed at all. On top of that, it was only a couple of miles from my house, which would be convenient for my kids.

In the meantime, we called multiple apartments and finally came across one that seemed to be a good fit. Casa Grande Apartments...it was right down the street from Samantha's house, and it was only $1,265 a month with a $500 deposit. We scheduled to take a tour at 1pm.

Next on the agenda: d...d...divorce attorney.

I forced myself to dial the first number. 949-225-4419. Nicholas Buscemi. I had no idea who he was, but his website talked about helping people in need. I was definitely in need...but all I got was a voicemail.

I kept dialing and dialing until I finally got someone on the line.

"Rancho Family Law, this is Caroline."

"Hi Caroline...um...my name is David...and uh...I had a few questions about getting divorced."

My hesitancy was met with an explanation of words I'd never encountered...like stipulated judgment, ex parte declaration, bifurcation of marriage...and the list goes on. I was taking furious notes trying to catch the gist of what this well-seasoned secretary was rattling off.

The main thing that stuck out was the $3,000 fee and the fact that it could take up to six months.

Caroline schooled me on "divorce 101," but I really wanted to talk with an *actual* attorney. So, I kept calling.

"Jarvis and Krieger, may I help you?"

"Yes, I have some questions about a divorce. Is there an attorney I can speak with?"

"Absolutely, let me transfer you to Scott Jarvis. One moment please…"

Scott was a confident man who seemed to be in his 30's. He was quick to answer every one of my questions, and he sounded like a bulldog when it came to getting the job done. He was *exactly* what Samantha was looking for. I booked an appointment for us to go see him on Wednesday.

By the time we grabbed some lunch, it was time to meet the property manager at Casa Grande. The massive complex was filled with tan-colored, pseudo Mexican-styled, two-story apartments with carports that stretched as far as my eye could see. The woman guided us down a windy path of sidewalks that eventually led to the stairs of unit #440.

As we walked into the tiny, one-bedroom apartment, my nostrils were filled with the smell of fresh paint and cheap carpet. After a three minute tour that included the living room / kitchen combo, a bedroom with one window, a spacious walk-in closet, and the single-sink bathroom, we both looked at each other with a glimmer in our eye.

"It's perfect," I whispered in her ear. She smiled back in agreement.

"We'll take it!" we said in unison.

"Okay…well, we *will* need you to fill out an application, and I'll have to check your income to ensure that everything looks fine. If everything is good, when would you like to move in?"

"Today…yes, today if possible."

It sounded like an insane request, but why not ask? I didn't exactly want to stay a second night at the Peacock Motel. If there was any possible way we could get into that apartment, I wanted to make it happen.

Since I hadn't seen my kids in a few days, I arranged with Laura to hang out with them for the afternoon. Although my five year old, Emerson, acted as nothing was different, my nine year old, Waverly, was feeling the pain. I took them to a local park to play bocce ball, and we had a fun time hanging out. The fun ended when I had to drop them off. The sight of my daughter running into her room crying because her Dad wasn't going to be there to tuck her in was unbearable. I turned around and walked out. It's all I could do. I couldn't stand there and feel the pain. There was no way.

A new wife…and a new life…were developing down the street, and I needed to get things set up.

Everything came together for us to move into the apartment so I ended up hauling my black garbage bags up the flight of stone stairs that evening. By the time I arrived, Samantha had already brought over an air mattress, sheets, and the blankets off of her bed. As I walked in, I noticed a yellow sheet of lined paper on the kitchen counter. It read…

My Love – welcome home!

We make quite a team. Right now you are with your children, and my heart is with you. My prayer is that tonight was better than you had hoped. This is a new season for you as a father, and I know that Waverly and Emerson are going to see a brand new Daddy. One who is fully present, who loves them unconditionally. You are an amazing man, David Trotter.

I love you with my heart and soul. I am so honored to spend the rest of my life with you. I will be missing you tonight. I will be thinking of you. I will call you as soon as I can. It is probably

going to be a long night for both of us. I can't wait to be in your
arms tonight.

I love you,
Samantha

After I regained my breath from her words of love, I waited with anticipation for her arrival. She arranged for Ben to stay at their house while
she joined me over at our new apartment. Once she finally arrived after
tucking her kids into bed, we drove down the street to Target for the es-
sentials. You don't think of everything you take for granted until it's not
there. Hand soap, paper towels, toilet paper, q-tips, and on and on. As
we were walking the aisles filling up our basket, I noticed that she was
heading for the men's section.

"Babe, have you ever thought about wearing some boxers?"

"Uh…nope…not gonna happen." I could see where this was going. I
had a feeling my tighty-whities were not up to par in her book, and she
was ready to make some changes in my life.

First the flip-flops and now this. What's next?!? Frankly, I didn't care. I
was willing to go anywhere she wanted to take me.

"How about these? *These* are cute." She was holding a three-pack of
darkly colored cotton briefs…something I would have never envisioned
wearing. I had worn white briefs my entire life…except for that period
when young boys enjoy the right of passage called "Underoos." Boxers
were never an option, because I like to feel like everything is secure
down there. Colored briefs just seemed a little…well…a little out on
the edge.

"Let's get these. You'll look great in them!"

How could I argue with that? My new woman wants me to ditch the
white underwear and start wearing some colors. Heck, let's give it a try.
We must have spent $300 that night. The nice part is that she just put it

on her card so Ben could pay for it.

After unpacking our purchases, I blew up the air mattress and changed into my new black underwear. I assumed that Samantha approved by the pinch on my left cheek as I passed her on the way to our comfy, plastic bed.

Tuesday, March 11th, 2008

Once again, I woke up to a kiss from Samantha as she headed out the door to go wake her kids and get them packed up for school. My mind started searching for a schedule of the day's activities, but there was nothing to be found. I didn't have appointments with church leaders or sermons to write or complainers to respond to. The only thing I needed to do was get some stuff from my house to move into the apartment.

Laura was willing to let me have the armoire, a metal dresser, TV, refrigerator, couch, and lamps. It was our previous furniture that we used to turn our "finished" garage into a playroom for the kids. I rented a moving truck and picked up a day laborer to give me a hand. By the time the sun was setting, our new "home" was complete with everything a newly hitched couple would need...except for a real bed and a dining room table.

Samantha came back to the apartment after making dinner for her family, and she brought a few things along with her...more clothes, cooking utensils, and a few pots and pans.

We went out to dinner that night, and my credit card became our source of income once again. Every night was becoming a perpetual "date night" with the love of my life. No kids to bathe or put to bed...no venting from my wife about how tired she was...and best of all...no stress from leading a church.

We came back to the apartment, curled up on the couch with a bowl of Samantha's favorite Thrifty ice cream, and we stared in each other's eyes as we talked. We talked and talked and talked. I agreed to Samantha's idea of not having a TV in our bedroom, and on top of that, we didn't even order cable for the TV in the living room. She didn't want it to be a distraction that would leave us staring at a source of light while we just sat next to each other on the couch.

We simply talked...and it was magical. I learned about her childhood, her hidden talents, and her love for life. She was like a fine gem that was waiting to be discovered. With every word that came out of her mouth, I felt like I was falling deeper and deeper in love.

"I've never talked this much in my life," she said.

"You and Ben don't talk about your day and what's going on in life?"

"Not really. He doesn't talk. I mean...he talks, but he never talks about anything other than where and when the kids need to be somewhere."

She was enamored by my desire to truly know her, and our evening ended the same way it had the previous four nights.

As she crawled back into bed, she cuddled up next to me. She took my arms and wrapped them around her as she nestled her face into the curve of my neck. Her chest pressed against mine. I had dreamed of holding her like this...the closeness...the connectedness. The intimacy of holding a woman I loved this close as I fell asleep. It was magical I tell you... it was magical.

Wednesday, March 12th, 2008
After awaking to another soft kiss, I showered and thought through the day ahead. Samantha was busy with her kids all day until we met with the divorce attorney mid-afternoon. This was a great opportunity for me to check my email and start getting aggressive on a job search.

Since we hadn't ordered Internet service yet, I thankfully found an open network that was accessible from the edge of our living room right by the balcony. I sat down to login.

The password to my Revolution email account had already been changed, but I regularly used another email from my blog with my own URL. Although I had received an immediate reply on Friday from my mom and dad, I had not responded nor had I checked my email for a few days.

Boy, was I surprised...I had a barrage of emails, and my RSS reader was full of blog posts about *my* life! Among the comments left on my blog, one person wrote under the name "John the Baptist"...

> *"I hope you and that fucking whore rot in hell."*

Although I never could have imagined John the Baptist saying something such as that, I guess it *is* possible. I clicked on the name to see if someone was stupid enough to leave their email address...and they were. The vitriolic words flowed from the keyboard of a nationally known author and Christian leader who I had recently met at a denominational leadership conference. My heart began to pound with anger and sadness as I clicked to "delete" the comment. Although the words disappeared from my blog that morning, they didn't disappear from my heart.

As I read through my RSS feeds, I saw that one blogger wrote...

> *David Trotter resigned over an affair with another women from his church. He also left his wife and children, and turned his back on his calling - apparently because it was all about him in the first place. Which, for those of you who read my blog, is the main problem I have with the hypocrites who run so many of America's churches. I am really not surprised - He was all about branding his name. It was all over the web. There was even a DavidTrotter. com for a while, but its gone now, he's left to follow his heart... Apparently after ripping the hearts from the chests of his followers.*

Another woman, who I had helped along in her faith journey, posted...

> *"I know, DT, that you are reading these blogs and that you don't care. And that is sad. When did your heart turn to stone? Are you proud? You are no longer a Revolutionary or a Christ follower. You have now become a DT follower. You say that you are with*

the Lord and you are following His way? Where in the Bible does it say to leave your wife, leave your kids, and start an adulterous affair? That is not God you are following, that is the devil!"

Yikes! I didn't anticipate the undesired publicity. The first guy was absolutely right. I did love publicity, and I sought it regularly for Revolution Church...not so much for my own name as far as I can remember. (By the way, my URL isn't davidtrotter.com...it's davidtrotter.tv...get it right.)

I kept hearing the same thing over and over in my heart, "Don't respond, David...don't defend yourself. Show restraint."

I didn't respond, but I did keep reading. Emails and blog posts started pouring in from people I led to faith in Jesus to people I had never even met before. They varied from hateful outbursts to pain-filled, honest comments like this post from Terry, who I helped through his overdose on speed...

> *I am devastated. I am just stunned and confused. The only other time I have felt like this was after Hurricane Andrew destroyed my neighborhood. That same feeling as I stood there and first saw all the damage. The same stunned, sad and horrified feeling, except this one cuts the core of my soul. Wow. This will not destroy my faith, because my faith is anchored by God, not man. Anyway, hope will return and God will prevail. I will be praying for all involved. God is truly greater than this.*

I was happy to hear of his faith, and I knew that God would walk with him through the pain I had caused. I kept reading until I eventually came across the words of Michael, the Downey campus pastor who left a comment on someone else's blog. He left his name as BFM, a moniker that he uses for a nickname that he goes by..."Big Fat Michael"...

> *The sad truth is that he never thought he did anything wrong, he was always right...and anyone who gave him any kind of account-ability, encouragement, or critique would be met with the same*

smart ass arrogance that alienated so many of the people he was leading...and that mentality continues now. Ultimately, and by his own admission, David has no idea how to be in relationship with anyone. He is brilliant, creative, driven, and quirky however; in his own narcissism he sabotaged every relationship around him. For me, it boils down to this...He did it to himself. No one put the pressure on him but himself. More people encouraged him to spend time with his own family. Again, by his own admission... and I quote, "I am not motivated by the expansion of the kingdom of God...I am motivated by my two biggest fears...getting people to like me and not being good enough." No one, no matter how hard many of us tried could change his perception...because it was always about him.

The pain of reading the words of people who I served alongside and people I didn't even know was unbearable. I closed my laptop and exhaled with sadness. When my own vulnerable words, gifts, and talents were used against me, I just sat there in amazement. Frankly, I was blown away that people would even notice that I was gone. I thought people would be shocked and hurt, but I didn't anticipate the public displays of anger and attack that I experienced. People obviously needed a place to vent. Unfortunately, I was willing to read it all...kinda like rubber-neckin' to see that horrible accident on the side of the road.

I decided to get dressed and head to the gym to work out. It had been a few days, and I didn't want to get out of my routine. The adrenaline of the Stairmaster and the flow of sweat were a welcome distraction from the painful ricochet of my decision to leave my wife.

After a quick shower and lunch, it was time to meet Samantha at the office of Jarvis and Krieger. We pulled into parking spots next to each other and made our way to the stairwell. As we walked down the first step, I noticed a couple of piles of human feces in the corner and the smell of urine was pungent. No wonder this guy was cheaper than the rest. We opted to walk down through the parking lot to find our way to the front entrance.

As we stepped out of the rickety elevator onto the 4th floor, things started to look up…at least they had new paint and new carpet. As we walked into the waiting area, the environment started to actually feel like an attorney's office. Dark furniture, lots of legal books, and some new magazines on the side table.

"Maybe this place will be okay after all," I thought to myself.

We were quickly ushered into his office that overlooked the city of Long Beach. As we sat down, I began to explain our situation.

"Well…*here's* the deal…we've both left our spouses to be with each other, and we're here to find out a bit more about a divorce process." His eyes opened wider than saucers, but he quickly regained his professional composure.

"Okay…not a problem…let's talk through what this would entail." He began to guide us through the road to a divorce, and he was patient to answer all our questions. I had already been looking into a do-it-yourself divorce, but he strongly recommended that Samantha retain an attorney because Ben's orthodontia practice was involved.

Samantha readily whipped out her credit card to put down the $2,500 retainer, but I opted to dialogue with Laura about a congenial divorce that wouldn't require an attorney.

As Scott was drawing up the documents, he inquired, "By the way, what do you do for a living David?"

"Oh…let's just say it's a bit public, and I'd rather not get into it."

He had that "I'll-find-out-on-my-own" look on his face, and he went back to preparing Samantha's paperwork. We walked out of his office, and Ben would be served with divorce papers within days.

Thursday, March 13th, 2008
Earlier in the week, I received word from my mom that my parents

would be driving down from the Sacramento area to stay with Laura and the kids for a few days. They were to arrive on Thursday for an evening "let's-all-pray-together-because-our-pastor-left-his-wife-and-resigned" event at Revolution Church, but they wanted to meet with me earlier in the day for lunch. I offered them a chance to meet Samantha, but they declined as you can imagine.

As the day and time arrived, I was overwhelmed with emotion. I was going to be facing my parents – eye to eye – for the first time since I left my wife to pursue another woman. Not that something such as this would be taken lightly in any family, but in our family, this is on par with *murder*. You just don't get a divorce much less leave your wife to be with someone else.

I was definitely prepared for the worst. I was thanking God that we chose a public place…mainly for the sake of my own safety and so the waitress could function as an eyewitness to any violence. I headed to Black Angus, a relatively quiet steak house with large, head-high booths that could mask sobbing, name-calling, and anything else that may go down.

I walked in wearing my new flip-flops and darkly colored underwear… not that my parents could see the latter. In a weird way, I was feeling this empowerment to be a "new me" with my new clothes and a new direction in life. After the obligatory, forced hugs, we sat down at a table to place our order.

The waitress who was serving us that day had no idea what she was walking into. My mom and I selected something quickly, and my dad didn't even order. I opted for a salad…something I could move around and stare at if I needed a distraction.

"I'd like to begin by giving you an update on my life if you don't mind," I offered. I thought that it would be best if I went first in order to prolong their opportunity to start yelling.

I launched into a 30-minute monologue that was essentially a longer explanation of the original letter that I emailed to them on the day I left

Laura. My dad pursed his lips and wrinkled his brow in the same way that he did when I'd bring home a "B" on a report card.

I wasn't going to give in to the feelings of being the "little kid" any more though. I was done with that phase of my life, and I wanted to make that clear.

At one point, my dad summarized, "So, basically what you're doing is giving everyone the middle finger and doing whatever you want?"

He *actually* used the middle finger.

He put it up in the air right in the middle of the restaurant. I couldn't believe it. This was my dad…the guy who scolded me for saying "crap" once when I dropped a piece a furniture that we were moving when I was 10 years old.

"Dad, you may think I'm heading for a cliff, but I don't care." This is where I was going to draw the line in the sand. I was done with being the kid. I was ready to make a statement. "I'm 35 years old, and I can do whatever I want. It may not be the *right* thing to do, but I don't care. I'm sick and tired of doing the *right* thing. Let me run off the cliff and do what I want."

With his piercing eyes looking into mine, my dad said point-blank, "You are a prodigal. You're running away to do your own thing, and that's the *truth*."

"Call me whatever you want Dad, but *yes*, I'm a grown man, and I'll do *whatever* I want."

Not a tear was shed from my eye that day, and it felt good. Usually, I'd crumble inside and that little boy who longed to be approved of would do whatever it took in order to receive the affirmation. I was beyond that now. I was a man with freedom…and no one could stop me.

I knew my mom's heart was breaking, but there was nothing I could do.

She actually listened, and she sought to understand. Although I knew that she didn't agree, she wanted to know what was going on inside of me…rather than trying to correct my decisions or tell me how bad I was for making them.

My dad paid for lunch, and we walked out into the parking lot. With tears in their eyes, my parents told me how much they loved me. With the breeze blowing through my shirt and between my toes, I walked toward my car and exhaled a huge sigh of relief. I made it through.

I called Samantha, and I told her how powerful it felt to *finally* be my own person. She was overjoyed for me, and we celebrated together.

Developing a Routine and Making New Friends
With each passing day, Samantha and I finally filled up our apartment with needed items such as a bed and dining room table, and we also started to develop more of a routine. She woke up, got her kids ready for school, came back to our apartment, and prepared for the day. I'd go work out, click around online for a while, think about the future, and hang out with my kids a few times a week. In the afternoon, she'd pick her kids up from school, make dinner, put them to bed, and come back to the apartment. Several times a week, Ben would take care of the kids all afternoon and evening, and Samantha got to relax and hang out with me.

There were so many new things about our lifestyle that we were both simply trying to adjust to. One of them was the fact that most of our friends had now turned into confused enemies. Because many assumed that I was the pastoral leader who brainwashed his weak, female follower into running off, I was demonized and perpetually attacked. Within days of leaving, I changed my cell phone number and kept my whereabouts a secret from everyone…even my own mother. I had heard of people who were so angry that they were even insinuating a physical attack, and I didn't feel the need to recover from physical injuries as well.

Samantha, on the other hand, was seen as the weak woman who needed to be confronted and lured back to her family home. Her mother and two sisters were ready to take on that role, and the three of them worked hard

via phone and email to talk her into returning back to Ben. The more
they tried…the more angry she became. Essentially, all relationships between her and her family were cut off, and she was devastated.

In times when you choose to make a major "mid-life correction" as I
called it, you really find out who your friends are. Actually, you find
out who your friends aren't. There was one young girl who was willing
to step across the unseen line to call Samantha and continue the friendship…a gal name Shannon Stephens. This 20-something had gone on a
previous trip to India, and she just happened to living in the same apartment complex as Samantha and me. She was a volunteer music leader at
Revolution, and she was taking major flack for being in contact with us.
In fact, she was asked to step down from the music team, because her
willingness to hang out with us was becoming a distraction for members
of the church.

Although I hate to paint a broad brushstroke, the Christian community
is rather known for jettisoning people along the way. There isn't much
of a willingness to walk alongside someone when they are taking a path
that isn't within the normal boundaries of Christianity, as they happen to
define it. We were *no different.*

No one contacted me to seek to understand.
No one offered to listen to what I was wrestling with.
No one was open to offering assistance.

I had "blown it" in the biggest possible way in the eyes of Christian
culture, and I was *out.* Of course, people did continue to email angry
"words of wisdom" and post "advice" on their blogs. I finally shut
down my Facebook and MySpace accounts so that the angry outbursts
wouldn't come through those information hubs.

The one person that was willing to walk with me through the entire
process was Kirk, my friend who had walked through something similar
while he was pastoring ROCKharbor Church. He was unshakable in his
assertion as he said, "David, you can't sin your way out of my life." I
had never heard that statement before, but it resonated…maybe because

I was a *sinner* for the first time in my life. It's not as if I hadn't *sinned* before. Believe me, I have a long list of sins that begins with pride, anger, resentment, workaholism, and so on. But, my sins tended to be the acceptable ones within Christian culture…oftentimes even rewarded.

Kirk and I would talk a few times a week, and he simply listened to what I was experiencing. He'd take time to ensure he heard what I was saying, and he'd update me on his life and activities. At no point did he offer advice or try to fix me. He knew that I was on my own path and that I wasn't interested in him telling me how to get back on the "right" one.

During one particular conversation, he mentioned in passing, "Oh by the way, Ron Latimore wanted me to tell you, 'Hello.'"

"Ahhh…I've been thinking about him a bit."

"I bet you have. You guys have something in common now," as Kirk pointed out the obvious.

What was obvious was the fact that Ron left his wife a couple of years back to be with another woman. Although this may not be *that* strange in our culture, it *was* out of the norm seeing as though Ron was one of the five founding men who helped Kirk start ROCKharbor Church.

In fact, I was the guy who happened to *out* Ron and his new beauty the previous year. I was sitting in a Starbucks working on a sermon for Easter Sunday when I saw an unmistakably muscular, African-American man walk into with a beautiful white woman on his arm. Immediately, I knew that it was Ron, and I somewhat recognized the woman…yet she definitely wasn't his wife, who had more of a motherly figure to her. After I asked what they were up to and I received an awkward answer, I immediately called Kirk with concern. Sure enough, Ron was planning his escape route from wife number one to make his way to wife number two.

Oddly enough, I found myself in the same situation now.

Later that week, I gave Ron a call, and I updated him on my story, and he was flabbergasted. He never thought I'd do something like that, but he was willing to walk with me. Ironically, he and his new wife, Rachel, had met Samantha a year prior when we ran into them at the Orange County Fair on a date night with our spouses. Worlds were colliding in a very positive way for all of us now.

Ron and Rachel were excited to meet Samantha once again, and we set a date for us all to get together for dinner. Their willingness to hang out with us and even have us over to dinner with their friends was an investment that we needed during a tremendously painful transition, but I couldn't help but think we were forming the "I Left My Wife Club."

You've got to know that our first few weeks together were absolutely "heaven on Earth" in many ways. I was *finally* experiencing the freedom that I had longed for, and the level of support and intimacy with Samantha was something that I had only dreamed of. We spent so much time simply enjoying one another, and I had never done that with another woman. Combine all that with the fact that the stress of leading a growing church had been completely removed.

On the other hand, it was sheer "hell" at the same time. The persistent attacks via email and word of mouth were disconcerting and heartbreaking. I never wanted to hurt anyone, but I realized how devastating my actions were to those I loved. I barely had any relationship with my parents, and there were no friends willing to walk with me except for Kirk and Ron. *Everyone* was gone.

On top of that, my wife and kids were melting down day by day. As I'd pick up the kids from our family home to spend time with them, I began to see Laura's weight severely drop. I had never seen her this skinny and even gaunt, and the look of anger and grief on her face each time I arrived was unbearable. I did my best to be upbeat and professional in my tone, but her pain was leaking out everywhere. Every conversation we had about the kids' schedule was tenuous.

"Do you even realize what you're doing to them?" she asked.

"What are you talking about?" I knew what she was alluding to, but I tried to dodge the bullet.

"What am I *talking* about? Are you *serious*?" She closed the front door and took a step outside. "You're killing your kids! Emerson is confused about where his dad is, and Waverly is bawling her eyes out every night because you've run off with Samantha."

"I understand." I tried to calm the situation, but nothing worked. "I'm doing the best I can right now."

"The *best* you can? Ha!" She was getting visibly angry with a vein beginning to bulge from her forehead. "I can't believe this!"

Although I had never had an angry exchange with her through this entire process, I was ready to launch a grenade back in her direction....in a calm vindictive voice.

"Here's the deal, Laura. I'm now going to be the father that you always wanted me to be. I'm going to be a great dad, and you're going to watch it all."

Her eyes became fierce with intensity as she simply said, "I hate you." And she kept going, "I hate you, I hate you, I HATE YOU!"

My lips formed into a smirk, and she walked inside and slammed the door behind her. Even though I intentionally stirred up her pain, it was brutal to know that my kids were now feeling the devastating effects of my decisions.

The distressing thing was that Samantha was experiencing the same thing on her end. On days that were tough for me, she'd hold me in our bed and console me with her closeness. On days that were tough for her, she'd curl up on the couch and close her eyes tightly shut. I'd wrap my arms around her and remind her that kids are resilient and they'll get through all this. In those moments, she wouldn't even talk...she just kept her eyes shut and cried. These were usually those nights when Ben was completely taking care of the four kids, and she missed them tremendously.

After several of these "closed eye" experiences, I began to notice her unwillingness to process whatever it was that she was feeling. She would shut down into a fetal position and close out everyone in the world... including me. I finally started saying, "Samantha, don't shut me out. I'm here for you. We're walking through the fire together just like we talked about. We'll get through this."

One night in particular, Samantha had a *complete* meltdown. As she cried on the couch for upwards of an hour, I continued to assure her and remind her of all the great things about our life together as well as how the kids were going to benefit from our great marriage.

As tears gushed from her eyes, she finally broke out of her shell, "I just can't take it anymore. I'm *dying* inside, because I can't be with my kids all the time. I feel *horrible* about them."

"Samantha, *look* at me!" I grabbed her face with my hands, and I stared at her tightly closed eyes. "*Open* your eyes!"

She wouldn't open them. She just looked away.

By this time, I was really starting to freak out inside. Was she thinking about leaving? Was she going to walk away from our relationship when we had committed to "walk through the fire" together? I couldn't let that happen. I leveraged everything to be with her, and I wasn't going to let her just walk away because she felt bad for her kids that night.

She grabbed her purse and tearfully said, "I just need to go for a drive to clear my head."

My abject insecurity caused my adrenaline to thrust me into action. It felt as though I was fighting for my life.

"Samantha, you are *not* just going to walk out that door without talking to me. We promised that we'd walk through the fire with one another, and we knew it was going to be hard. We knew that no one would walk with us, but we'd have each other. We counted the cost of putting our kids through this, but we committed to support each other in the process. Our kids will get through this, and God will help us find a way."

She sat back down on the couch, and her eyes finally started to open. She began to let me into her world. We began to talk things through, and we both settled down. After an hour or so of dialogue, she found a place of contentment.

"David, thank you for not letting me walk out that door. I'm not sure I would have come back if I drove away. I'm so glad I didn't do that. I want to be with you for the rest of my life, and I'm committed to you no matter what. I love you so much."

"I love you, too…"

Trying to Make a Living

As I continued to go to therapy once a week with Randy, I was trying to find my way through the daily challenges that would arise…one of which was my ability to make a living. Having been in professional ministry as a pastor in a local church for 10 years, I knew it was going to be difficult to find something that would pay beyond $35,000.

Although I had CEO-level skills and experience, who wants to hire a guy who has worked in a church most of his adult life? I did have three years of experience working at a paper distribution company, but that was right out of college. It probably wouldn't count for much.

After consulting with Randy and Kirk, everyone was of the opinion that it probably wouldn't be a good idea to just go out and get a job. For one, I probably wouldn't make that much. And, number two, I'd die. I'd absolutely *die* working for someone at a 9-5 job where I wasn't able to express my gifts of leadership, communication, and creativity.

Instead, I needed to figure out something to do on my own.

The only thing I could think of at the time was to start a "consulting" business where I could coach people with my gifts of strategy and vision. I started to envision the possibility of helping leaders get a handle on the direction of their church or business. Or, maybe I could coach someone through a life transition. I know it sounds a little ironic that I'd be the one coaching another person through a major life transition, but I had to find a way to use my gifts and generate income.

I was like the Tommy Lasorda of relationships. I may not be able to run the bases myself, but I can surely tell you how to do it.

Since the theme of a "revolution" was at the core of my being, I started to develop a simple website with the URL of www.startarevolution.tv. Through the written content and a simple video I produced, I offered to help people get "unstuck" from where they were lacking freedom and find a strategic path that would revolutionize their life and leadership.

After launching the site, I drafted an email announcing my new venture and my availability to help anyone who may be interested. I compiled a list of over 300 emails of friends from Revolution and church leaders around the country. I knew that I'd get massive flack for offering my services...especially with a name that used the term "revolution."

I didn't care. People already hated me, so a little more hatred wasn't going to make a difference. All I needed was one person to give me a chance...one person. That's all I needed.

I ran the email past Samantha, and I clicked "send." Within a matter of minutes, I received responses like...

> *"You've got to be kidding!"*
> *"I can't believe you're even thinking about this."*
> *"Remove me from your list immediately."*

Let's just say that the response was less than positive. Yet, there was one person who emailed me back with an openness to connect...a man named John Weeks.

I met John at Revolution in the previous year as his ex-wife and kids brought him to church. He was an odd sort to say the least. Always drinking coffee and little slumped over with his jeans hanging below where they should. I ended up burying his son during the previous summer after his son's car ran off the road resulting in his death. It was a painful time for the family as you can imagine, and I had the privilege of walking with them through the experience...but I never really got to know John.

His email simply said...

> *David – I have several ideas that I'd like to share with you. I could use your help in getting one of them started. Are you available for lunch? John*

This was exactly what I was looking for...one person who would give me a chance! I emailed him back immediately, and we set a date for lunch. This middle-aged man who practically appeared homeless drove a beat-up Dodge van that was white when it was originally sold. Come to find out...he started a company six years prior that was now selling over $13 million in Halloween costumes and pool supplies. Yes, it was an odd combination, but he found a way to do it. This guy was a mad scientist who knew how to make money.

What ensued was a multi-week conversation about how to launch a website for tweens that would be similar to Facebook. We researched the competition, developed a business plan, and started to raise investment money from his business friends.

It kept me busy, and I felt like I had hope for the future while my expenses were starting to rack up on my credit card.

Therapy, Church, and Taking More Risks

Not only did I have hope in the area of business, but therapy was going well, too. I kept talking about my desire for "intimacy" with each session, and Randy pushed me to find it. Although I talked about Samantha constantly, he never really ventured into that territory. He kept things centered on friends and my kids, and I had a feeling why.

As a Christian therapist, he was definitely in a precarious place by continuing to counsel me in the midst of my decision. It could be construed that his support was actually a voice of approval in my life, but I knew it wasn't.

I knew that he didn't necessarily approve of what I was doing.

"David, I've been thinking about our time together. You've got to know that I've thought long and hard about continuing to see you. Your dad called me this week and questioned me on why I continued to help you. He was definitely not in agreement with my actions."

"*Really?* He called you?" I was quietly surprised that my dad was going to the extent of contacting my therapist. He was obviously desperate to send a reverberating message through my life.

"Yes, and I told him that I'd continue to help you." I could see the resolve in his face. "Here's my thought. If you're going to start a new life and marriage with Samantha, I can't stop you. Yet, if you're going to head that direction, I want you to have the best marriage possible. I'm committed to you and your growth in this process."

The relief and support I felt in that moment were so soothing. I knew that he was with me no matter what. He had my best interest in mind... even if I was straying down a path into uncharted territory.

"You also need to know that your dad was contacted by Samantha's uncle. Somehow this guy in Oklahoma found your Dad online and called him at his office. He threatened to send his *police friends* out to California to take her back and take care of you as well."

"Great...that's just what I need...someone else coming after me."

As I walked out of his office that day, I shook it all off and knew that I had to stay the course no matter what. Nothing and no one was going to stand in the way of me getting the kind of life that I wanted deep down inside.

As part of my continued growth, I definitely wanted to stay connected to God. Despite all the emails and blog posts about my choice to turn and follow Satan, I just didn't sense that at all. In fact, I sensed the opposite. I was feeling close to God and His Divine Presence more and more.

On most evenings, Samantha and I would lay in bed and read Scripture to one another and spend some time praying together. We asked God for wisdom and strength in the process. From time to time, we'd discuss what God thought about our whole ordeal, but we never came to an understanding. We knew that our choice to leave our spouses wouldn't be something God was excited about. Yet, if we developed a strong, loving marriage, at what point would God approve or bless us? After we got married? After five years? Or…never?

We didn't know, but we wanted to keep growing in our faith so we prayed together and attended church every Sunday. Most weeks, we drove 30 or so minutes up to Los Angeles to avoid encountering anyone we would know to attend Mosaic Church, which met at a local nightclub called The Mayan. We remained anonymous as we walked in and out, but it was nice to be in a corporate worship service with other followers of Jesus. Samantha and I would hold hands and enjoy connecting with God together. The rush of being with her in a church setting was now a weekly experience I looked forward to.

This 'new life' as I called it felt like one risk after another. I was probably considered a rather adventurous person before all of this, but I never really felt that way. I wanted more adventure and excitement in my life, and I wanted to feel the freedom of doing new things.

From working out daily to trying new food to wearing colored underwear, I was *really* starting to love this new life of freedom and risk. I know it sounds a bit ridiculous, but I had been doing what was right, practical, and strategic for upwards of 35 years. I was so driven toward my goals that I never stopped to enjoy the moment…ever.

After getting home from a workout one morning, I looked in the mirror at my body. Having lost 20 pounds, my stomach was starting to shrink and muscles that I hadn't seen since college were re-appearing. I looked down at my nakedness, and I saw a bright-white torso and two shining feet. I was sick of avoiding the beach because of my pudgy whiteness and calf-high sock lines from never allowing the sun to shine upon my virgin toes.

I was going to do something about this. Earlier that week, I noticed a tanning salon near the grocery store, and I began to wonder what that experience would be like. I could darken this torso and finally get rid of these sock lines. I could make the move to ankle socks like everyone else I knew, and I would finally get rid of these tan lines that created an arbitrary division of my body.

I walked right in…sweating and nervous.

After a few questions were answered and I slapped down my credit card, I found myself walking into a small room with an upright tanning booth. I stripped down to my dark green underwear and placed the eye protection on my face.

"I can't *believe* I'm doing this," I whispered to myself. "If my wife could see me now, she'd be laughing her head off. Dave Trotter getting into a tanning booth."

Well, I did. I walked right in, cranked up the music, and stood there for five minutes. The warmth that enveloped my body with the sound of invigorating music was like a bath for my soul. I didn't want the peaceful moments to go away. I loved the feeling of being alone in a tight space with light shining all around me.

After several sessions, I was seeing the results that I wanted, and I was ready to make the big switch...the switch from the old-school, calf-high white socks to the black ankle socks that Samantha was dying for me to wear. With the sock lines finally gone, I slipped on my new footwear, and I felt like a new person.

All these changes were starting to rack up. It was as if I was becoming the person I always wanted to become, but I was too scared to be. It's amazing what a little tan and a pair of socks can do for a guy.

Planning for the Big Day

Our time before bed was so precious each evening. It was an intimate experience as we shared about our day and talked about our hopes and dreams for the future.

One particular evening, Samantha arrived back to our apartment after putting her kids to bed, and she had a stack of magazines in her hands. She joined me in bed and plopped down her load next to me...a multitude of periodicals on one subject...weddings.

"Wow, it looks like you're doing a little research," I said.

"Yeah, I'm excited about our *big day*, and it's never too early to start planning. I'm excited to pick out a new dress."

"I haven't even asked you to marry me yet!" I started laughing, and she punched me in the shoulder.

"I'm thinking we can get married in the backyard at my house in...June. How does that sound?"

"Um...sounds great! Will Ben be out by then?" I asked.

"Oh yeah. I'll make sure that happens." She started to laugh and kept flipping through each page envisioning how the backyard would be decorated.

We weren't exactly sure how many people would even come to the wedding, but we knew that it would be a great occasion. We started dreaming about the big day, and she even created an online profile on a wedding site for us to get the word out.

As the days went by, Samantha started hinting about the need for a new ring to signify our love for one another. I was hesitant about taking the step because of our finances, but it sure did seem like a fun idea.

We started browsing through magazines and high-end shops at Fashion Island in Newport Beach. We wondered if we sold her original wedding ring if that would make even a dent in the payment for another. Unfortunately, the diamond was so small and the design was so out of date that it didn't really amount to much.

We decided to venture up to LA to check out the diamond district for a great deal. After being overwhelmed with an endless stream of diamond salespeople, we finally made our way into Princess Jewelry, a business with a sweet Asian mother overseeing it all. Her son had recently taken over, and they offered custom-made rings with a great selection of diamonds.

They were helpful to work with, and I was starting to think that this could really be an option. After talking through an ultra-modern, platinum design with a 1.5 carat, princess-cut diamond for her and a simple, titanium band for me, we walked out of the store to take a breath.

"I'm just not sure about this, Samantha." I was nervous about spending so much money on my credit card when I had no idea when I'd ever start generating an income.

"I understand. If you don't feel comfortable with it, we don't have to do it." Her big, blue eyes stared up at me as she said, "But it is *gorgeous!*"

We walked back in the store, and I pulled out my credit card once again.

In his thick Asian accent, the man said, "The total will be $6,495, sir."

I swallowed deep and agreed to the purchase. The ring would be ready within two weeks.

With the purchase of her engagement ring, Samantha was becoming more and more uncomfortable with the fact that her divorce was in process and mine was not. Her displeasure generally surfaced through a bout of pouting on the couch as she flipped through wedding magazines. After I'd pick up on the downward spiral of her emotions, I'd quickly ask, "Honey, what's wrong?"

"Oh, nothing. I'm *fine*."

This was the beginning of a cat and mouse game to tease out her true feelings and then manage her emotions for her. I took on the role of counselor on more than one occasion, and I started to grow weary of her massive mood swings. I was used to being the one who experienced the highs and lows in a relationship. Now the tables were turned. I had to deal with her roller coaster ride, and I was getting tired of hanging on.

"I just don't understand why you can't tell your wife that you're ready to get a divorce. Hire the attorney, and just get *going* with it."

I didn't want to see my wife hurting like she was. Frankly, her pain touched me. Any human being that's filled with any measure of compassion doesn't like to see someone else heartbroken. This wasn't just *any* person…this was my wife of 14 years and the mother of my children.

I tried to help Samantha understand my compassion. "I'm trying not to push Laura into this so quick, and I'd really rather not spend the money on an attorney."

"*Whatever*…I think you're just dragging your feet. Quit being so nice and just get it done." Unfortunately, she wasn't using a tone of voice that meant "whatever." I was going to pay for this later on.

Not only was she ready for me to get a move on with my divorce, but she had also requested that I get a *vasectomy*…something Laura had wanted me to do for years and something Ben had done a long time ago.

After using condoms for a week or so, I joined Samantha for an appointment at a local Planned Parenthood office for some free birth control. She didn't want to go through the embarrassment of going to her normal doctor and explaining why she was there. Unfortunately, the new birth control was now causing some bleeding, and she was ready to be done with the whole ordeal.

After a couple of weeks of going back and forth, I finally made the calls. With the phone shaking in my hand, I called Scott Jarvis to set up a time to sign the divorce paperwork, and I called my doctor to get a referral to a urologist. Two things that I never thought I'd ever do in my lifetime. That night, Samantha was *elated* to hear the news.

A Cold Place Called Chick-fil-a

By this time, the kids were growing accustomed to being with me and without their mom, and I started hanging out with Samantha's kids as well. In fact, since the kids had already known each other for years, we got all the kids together to hang out on several occasions...everyone except her oldest son, Nathan.

Nathan was not so keen on his mom's transition from Ben to me. He was angry about the entire situation, and he didn't want to have anything to do it.

It didn't help that he was in the car with his dad, Ben, as we passed each other going in opposite directions...while *I* was driving Samantha's SUV all alone. Through his dark sunglasses, I could feel Ben's piercing eyes as he raised up his middle finger and mouthed, "Fuck you."

What's up with me and the middle finger?
First my dad...and *now* Ben.

At least the other kids were dealing with the change as best as they could, and we had a great time when we were together.

On one occasion, Samantha was at a sporting event with Nathan, so I took the other five kids to Chick-fil-a for dinner. We loaded into Samantha's SUV, and I felt like the ultimate dad venturing out into public with the entire herd. As soon as we walked in to the restaurant, I noticed that there were a couple of women and their kids from Revolution who were finishing their meals. Although we had been close friends in the past, they completely avoided eye contact with me and left as soon as they could.

I shouldn't have expected anything different.

That's how I was being treated via email and blogs, so why would expect anything different in person? I did leave my wife and resign as the pastor of the church. I guess they were simply responding the only way their pain would allow them to.

The kids loved being together that night and on subsequent adventures as well…from a spaghetti dinner on our patio to swimming in our pool to buying a fish tank with everyone getting to choose his or her own fish. It was exhilarating to get a glimpse of life with six kids as we hung out together…everyone except Nathan.

The excitement of the adventure would soon come to a crashing halt when I'd drop my kids back off at the house. I would walk through the front door with their backpacks in hand to see subtle changes each time I arrived.

A new screen door. A cabinet removed from the wall where I used to store my keys and wallet. And a new family photo hung in its place… without *me* in it.

Shelley Pelosi, the part-time Revolution Communications Director who repeatedly attacked me online, offered to take their photos at the beach in exchange for putting them on iStockphoto. Of course, the one that Laura chose to hang by the front door was of the three of them walking away from the camera…holding hands…looking over their shoulders back at the camera.

As I looked at the photo, I could just hear Laura saying, "Byyye Dave! We're walking away from you…this is our new family."

And, almost every time I dropped the kids off, Laura asked for the house key back. It was obvious that she regretted giving it to me on the night Samantha and I returned from San Diego...but I didn't want to give it back. It was still *my* house, too.

My heart sunk knowing that I wouldn't be tucking them into their own bed or praying for sweet dreams or be available in the middle of the night.

Daddy wasn't there.

Friday, April 11th, 2008
After some planning and the completion of her engagement ring, the day arrived for us to spend a romantic evening together with the plan of exchanging vows. Although our divorce process wouldn't allow us to get legally married for another six months or so, we knew that we were truly married in our hearts.

I booked a room overlooking the ocean, and I made reservations at a neighboring restaurant. Samantha was to meet me on a bench right by the water, and we would begin our evening together. Although she was an hour late because of getting lost, her arrival was unbelievable. Her new shimmering, silk, strapless dress showed off her wondrous curves as she walked down the path.

She sat down beside me, and I handed her an ear bud from my iPod... something we had done in India. "Just listen," I said.

> *I want to live like there's no tomorrow.*
> *I want to dance like no one's around.*
> *I want to sing like nobody's listening.*
> *Before I lay my body down.*
> *I want to give like I have plenty.*
> *I want to love like I'm not afraid.*
> *I want to be the man I was meant to be.*
> *I want to be the way I was made.* [3]

As the song finished, I looked her in the eye, and I said, "This is how you make me feel. This is the type of adventurous life of freedom that you inspire me to. I love you more than you'll ever know."

I went on to espouse my love in every way I could imagine. I pulled out her diamond ring from my pocket, and I asked, "Will you marry me?"

"Absolutely." We slid it on her finger, and she kissed me tenderly.

She pulled out a five page, hand-written note from her pocket, and she began to read it word for word. She began by re-capping our experiences in India and with each portion she ended with, *"That day I gave you a piece of my heart."* I was getting chills from head to toe as the woman of my dreams poured out her heart about her love and admiration of me.

> *We came home, and in 11 days, I had decided that I wanted to spend the rest of my life with David Trotter. I am ready to walk away from 15 years of history, a safe marriage with no conflict. I am ready to walk through the fire to be with you, for the rest of our lives. Tonight I give you my whole heart. I promise to love you everyday of my life.*
>
> *I promise to serve you. I promise to never go to bed angry. I promise to communicate and try not to go inside. I promise to love Waverly and Emerson like I love my own children. I promise to support you and cheer you on. I promise to work hard at our marriage to make it successful. I promise to never quit on you. I promise to give you all of me. I love you. I love you in a way I didn't know was possible. I don't want to live this life without you.*
>
> *David Trotter, will you be my partner for life?*
> *Will you be my husband?*

Standing in my shoes at the water's edge, I was completely consumed with her love. I accepted her invitation of a life together, and she slid the ring on my finger. This night symbolized the beginning of our new life together.

Thursday, April 17th, 2008

A week later, things were now truly setting into a routine. I was starting to work on a couple of business projects, and I was trying to make new contacts each day. Through my friend Kirk, I had developed a connection with a guy named Dyno...that's all he went by.

On the day Dyno and I planned to have lunch together, I woke up feeling a bit funky. In the six weeks that Samantha and I had lived together, I felt very secure about our relationship and her commitment to me. Yet, on that morning, something felt *different*.

The night before had been great. We enjoyed a wonderful walk around the block together. We had a passionate experience making love to one another as we did every evening, and we fell asleep in each other's arms.

She kissed me good-bye that morning, and everything was as "normal" as normal could be in this new life.

Yet, I felt queasy. On my drive to lunch with Dyno, I gave her a call to re-assure myself.

"Hey babe...how did the morning go with the kids?"

"Great. Everything went fine." She sounded normal.

"Hey...um...I gotta tell you...I feel kinda weird about you being at your house today. Is everything okay?"

"Yeah, of course everything is fine." She re-assured me, but I still felt uneasy.

"What do you want to do tonight?" I asked.

"Well, I'm not sure...maybe a walk on the beach after dinner. How does that sound?"

"I *love* the sound of that!"

"Just give me a call after your lunch, and we'll talk about our plans."

I felt better just hearing her voice. She had soothed any concern I had, and I walked into Fortune Cookie to have lunch with Dyno. We got to know one another, and I gave him an update on the transitions I was experiencing in life. We talked about some business and ministry opportunities and planned to stay in touch.

I hopped back in my car to head back to the apartment, and I gave Samantha a call. I re-dialed her number, and all I heard was a buzzing sound on the other end. I figured something got connected weird, so I re-dialed her number again.

"Were sorry you have reached a number that has been disconnected or is no longer in service, if you feel you have reached this recording in error, please hang up and try your call again."

My worst nightmare was happening.
I felt like something just wasn't right…but now I knew for sure.

Samantha just shut her eyes.

BLACK THURSDAY

chapter six

It was as if someone had just punched me in the stomach…my breath was taken away. I knew what had happened, and I headed straight back to our apartment.

One hand was tightly gripping the steering wheel while the other began to tap the side of it furiously. My body started rocking back and forth in the driver's seat as I hoped that my hunch earlier that morning was wrong. As every light turned green, my foot would press down on the gas faster and farther…trying to get there as quickly as I could.

Mid-way home, my phone rang, and it was John Weeks – the only guy who answered my startarevolution.tv email without hate.

"Hey Dave, how ya doin'?"

"Uh…fine John." My breathing was fast and labored…as if I had just run a 40-day-long marathon. "I'm doing okay." I was lying.

"Good, well then…" John shot off into an update on the project we had been seeking investment money toward, but it just morphed into back-ground noise like a television blaring while reading that "just-arrived-and-I'm-ruining-your-life" email.

"Dave? *Dave?*"

"Huh, what's up?"

It was as if he was waking me up from a trauma-induced coma. I tried to carry on the conversation, but I just couldn't. Maybe God sent John's call as a way to distract me from completely melting down while I drove.

With John on the other line, I still had the phone stuck to my ear as I bounded up the stone steps that led to our front door...the front door that Samantha and I had walked through day after day for the past six weeks.

My hands were shaking so bad I could barely fit the key into the lock. I opened the door, and my worst nightmare had come true.

A note from Samantha was lying on the dining room table...and her diamond ring and necklace were on top of it.

"John...I gotta go...I gotta go."
John had no clue what was going on, and I just hung up the phone.

One sheet of white, lined notebook paper was tossed on the table...the kind you used in high school or college to take notes on. The kind that was disposable, cheap, and worthless...torn from a spiral notebook with fragments still hanging off on the left.

My eyes started to quickly scan through Samantha's hand-written words scrawled out with a pencil...

David,

I need to share my heart with you. I have been wrestling inside for a couple of weeks now. I feel so much guilt for tearing apart my family. Guilt that I can no longer live with. The way you love me and know me is what kept me going. I made promises to you that I can no longer keep. I am sorry.

You left everything that was safe to be with me. I am sorry. I am sorry that we could not have been together under different circumstances. I hope to some day forget the way you make me feel. I hope that you will find someone that will love you the way you need to be loved.

I am sorry I couldn't stay. I am sorry I couldn't keep those promises. I am sorry for what this now means for your life. <u>Please</u> don't fight for me. I can't come back again. I do love you. I do believe in you. You have a beautiful mind, and you have an amazing heart. I will miss not being a part of your life. That is what is going to be the hardest for me. I will miss being your friend. I will miss you!

Samantha

P.S. I will try and send you some money.

As the note dropped from my shaking hand onto the table, my head turned to the right as I stared through the hallway into the walk-in closet. The door was open, and I could see that her half of the closet was completely empty. All of her clothes were gone. I rushed over to her side of the bed, and the stack of wedding magazines, her iPod, and Bible were nowhere to be found.

"*Shiiiiiit!* What the *fuck* just happened?!?"

My heart started pounding faster and faster, and my head was shaking back and forth. As I picked up the phone, there was only one person I thought of calling. I dialed Kirk's number, and my mind was frantically searching for a way to fix all this.

My voice was furious with intensity, and I couldn't get the words out fast enough.

"Kirk, she *left*. Everything is *gone*. I came home from lunch with Dyno and there was a letter and her ring and her necklace and all her stuff is *gone*."

I just kept talking and talking like a senseless lover who just lost his wife in a tragic accident.

"Okay. Settle down. I'm here with you." Kirk was starting to talk me off the ledge. He had been there before. He knew what it was like.

"Fuck, fuck, fuck, *FUCK!*"

I wasn't one to drop the f-bomb on many occasions since it didn't seem to resonate too well with my straight-as-an-arrow, Christian upbringing, but now was the time if ever. In fact, it's about the only word I could get out of my mouth.

"I'm gonna go over there and try to talk some sense into her! I'm going over there right *now!*"

"Okay...I'll stay on the line with you...okay?"

"Um...yeah..." I was already in the zone...trying to figure out what I was going to say to her. I rushed out the door and headed to my car.

"Do you want me to come up there to be with you?" Kirk asked.

"Yeah, that would probably be good...but just stay on the line if you can."

I have no clue what Kirk and I were talking about while I drove to Samantha's house. I was a man on a mission to get the love of my life back...the woman who I had left *everything* for.

I pulled into her cul-de-sac and parked in front of her driveway to prevent her from leaving abruptly. With more adrenaline pumping through my veins than the time I was in a fistfight with Henry Barrett in elementary school, I headed straight for her front door.

KNOCK! KNOCK! KNOCK!

As Ben opened the front door, I demanded, "I want to see Samantha. Send her out here!" I backed away a bit to prevent him from taking a sucker punch...although I knew he didn't have it in him.

"You've done *enough* to tear apart our family. Leave or I'm calling the police!"

His threat meant nothing to me.

"Fine, call the police. Get them over here. I'll be right here on the sidewalk waiting for Samantha to come out."

He started dialing someone on his phone, but I seriously doubted that he was *really* calling the police. He wasn't man enough to do that.

By this time, I hung up on Kirk. I had to focus on Samantha. As I looked up toward the second story of her home, I called out at the top of my lungs, "Samantha! Samantha! I want to talk to you!"

After a moment, she emerged from the front door...no shoes, no makeup...with eyes that were tired and had been crying. She stood in front of me with her arms crossed.

I was *right*...she had closed her eyes.

As I pleaded with her to come back with me, her eyes slightly opened.

She said softly in way so that Ben couldn't hear, "David, stop. I can't. I can't wreck my family like this. I love you, but I just can't."

I used every tactic I could muster from my scattered mind. I feverishly brought up our commitment to "walk through the fire" together and all our promises to be with each other for the rest of our lives. My hands were fumbling and shaking so much that I dropped my sweaty phone mid-way through my begging. I quickly picked it up and popped the cover back on…continuing to remind her that I left *everything* to be with her.

Nothing worked. She just stood there…*eyes closed.*

By this time, Ben had walked over and was standing within 3 feet of us…off to the side…as if he was in the position of a mediator. He never said anything, but he just stood there and listened to me pleading for her to come back.

As I pointed at him, I asked her with the intensity of a left-behind lover, "Do you *seriously* want to be with this guy? You want to be with the guy who *you said* has *no adventure* in his body? You want to be with the guy who *you said* was *so boring* as I was making *passionate love* to you at least once a day for six weeks straight?!?"

"Stop! Stop, David! Quit saying these things!" she begged me.

I couldn't believe Ben just stood there and took every word. He didn't hit me, and I'm not even sure that he clinched his fists.

"What a wuss!" I said to myself.

What he did do was bend down to pick something up off the ground.

"You may need this," he said with a straight face. Ben handed me my cell phone battery that I didn't even realize was missing when I picked up the back to my phone earlier. What kind of guy has the wherewithal to think about my need for a cell phone battery as I stand there humiliating him in front of his wife?

Frankly, I exhausted every angle I knew. She wouldn't even look at me. All I could do was to launch one last ditch effort.

"I'm not going anywhere. I'm not going back to my wife. I'm waiting for you. I'll wait as long as it takes. You know how to reach me."

As I turned to walk back to my car, Samantha and Ben headed back inside. I started the engine, and I drove away with a sense that my life was completely over. I instinctively called Kirk back, and he was already on his way. In fact, he had even called Dyno to meet him at the apartment.

Standing in a Tomb

I turned the doorknob, and I walked back inside what was now nothing more than a tomb that held the memories of a dead relationship. I paced back and forth until Kirk could arrive. My mind was spinning, and I could barely form a clear thought.

After a knock at the door, I twisted the handle, and Kirk walked in. A manly fist bump wasn't going do under these circumstances, so I gripped him with a hug that said, "Thank God you're here."

I re-capped the day...from my awkward sense in the morning to her comforting re-assurance to the devastation of hearing the sound of a disconnected phone. He sat and listened as I paced back and forth practically wearing through the recently installed, cheap apartment carpet.

Dyno finally arrived, and he made it through the maze of carports and walkways to find the front door. They sat there and listened as I rambled on and on like that homeless guy that walks around aimlessly recounting the details of a life gone by...and yet has no place to go.

Words that I was accustomed to using just wouldn't suffice to describe the depth of agony I was feeling in that moment. The only word that seemed to encapsulate the loss, brokenness, and trauma was "fuck."

I kept saying it over and over and over...with no other words attached or in between.

"Fuck, fuck, fuck, FUCK!"

I said it with every possible annunciation...from long and drawn out in agony to quick and loud in anger. If there was an official representative on hand that day, I quite possibly could have set a Guinness world record for dropping the f-bomb the most times within 24 hours. A vindictive stream started to take over within me. I wanted to get back at her...or at least communicate my anger in some vengeful way.

"Maybe I should get plastic sandwich bags and put each kid's fish inside one with their names written on the side...leaving them on her front door step to die without water," I thought to myself.

In my better judgment, I started piling every object she had purchased within our apartment on top of the dining room tablecloth.

The dishes and silverware.
The pots and pans.
The towels.
The photos of us together.
Clothes that she had purchased for me.
Even the food from the refrigerator.

I didn't want *any* evidence of her presence to remain. I planned to wrap it all up in the tablecloth like a Santa-style sack and throw it across her front lawn.

Thankfully, Kirk and Dyno talked some sense into me.

"Bro, *stop!* Do you ever want a chance to be back with her?" Dyno wisely asked.

His question put the brakes on my craziness. "Yeah...of course."

"Then, why would you throw all that stuff on her lawn? Do you really think that's gonna help?"

Recognizing his wisdom, I slowed down the impromptu packing party and scrapped that plan. The flaming f-bombs started to subside, and reality began to set in.

What was I going to do? I doubt I would have ever left my wife if I knew that I would just end up all alone. It was because of Samantha that I walked away from 10 years in full-time ministry as a pastor and 14 years of marriage. What was I going to do *now?*

Kirk and Dyno suggested that they get me out of the apartment by heading to Palm Springs or Vegas for the weekend. While I was packing a bag, Kirk walked into our bedroom and noticed a framed photo of Samantha and I on top of the metal dresser.

"Is this her?" he asked. He had never met her...just heard me talk about her incessantly.

"Yeah...that's her."

He didn't say anything. I mean...what would a friend say in that situation? "Wow, she's hot" or "You guys look great together" or "She isn't that great...you don't need her." No matter what you say, it isn't going to help. That's why he didn't say anything.

The funny thing was...I realized that she wasn't that hot.

Within a matter of moments, it was as if the goggles I had been wearing weren't as powerful anymore. I was actually embarrassed for Kirk to see the photo of us together. All the things that I loved about her tarnished in that moment...yet she's all I wanted.

As he set the photo back in place, I kept packing my bag for the night. Before we headed out the door, I opened my laptop to send Samantha an email...

Hi Samantha,

I'm going out of town for a couple of days. If you want to come back to have an amazing, life-giving, courageous marriage, I will immediately return to be with you. I love you more than anyone or anything else in this world. My arms are wide, and my heart is open. I love you so much. I won't quit loving you. I'm wiling to do whatever it takes to be with you. I think I've already demonstrated that. I'll be waiting for your call.

Love always,
David

Having been in moment-by-moment contact with her for two months, I now felt like one of my own limbs was severed. Eleven minutes later, I sent a second email...

Hey Samantha,

I just can't seem to quit typing. I love you so much. I just want to be with you. I am committed...

To being the best husband you could ever have.
To being the best dad/friend or whatever you want me to be to your/our children.
To being the best friend you've always longed for.
To being the soul mate you've never had.
To being the most amazing lover you've ever experienced.

I love you more than oxygen. I want to be with you. Please return to me. I am committed.

Your soul mate and best friend,
David

We walked out of the apartment, and I shut the door to the tomb.

To Cry or Not to Cry

As we drove away from Cypress, I just couldn't see myself spending two or three days that far out of town, so we headed toward to a fancy hotel in Costa Mesa that would become a one-night refuge for my wounded soul. I was in a semi-comatose state as we pulled up to the valet station. Kirk took care of everything that evening...like one of those babysitters you see out in public with a group of "handi-capables" who need supervision.

He walked ahead to pay for the room while I stumbled behind him carrying my lone bag.

After making the necessary arrangements, we made our way up the elevator to our room. As we walked in, I dropped down on the bed. I couldn't think straight, and I really had nothing more to say. I had said it all.

I could feel myself wanting to cry...but I was too scared.

I hadn't shed a single tear that day, but I was afraid that if I actually crossed the line and started to cry...I may never come back. So, I sucked it up, and I just laid there.

"Do you want to watch TV?" Kirk asked.

"Whatever." I was too spent to even make that decision. I just wanted everything to go away.

Instead, we headed to Kirk's house for him to pack a quick bag for the night. As he was packing, Samantha *finally* called.

I paced back and forth under the streetlight outside of Kirk's house as I talked with her for over an hour that night. I tried everything within my power to woo her back to me...everything from talking about our commitment to one another to our great relationship to how much she disliked being with Ben.

"When you find yourself bored with his lack of adventure, I want you to think about me. When he doesn't pray with you, I want you to think about me. When you sit in the bottom of your closet and cry to yourself because he won't talk about life with you, I want you to think about me."

The brutal onslaught of manipulative statements just wouldn't stop flowing out of my mouth. At no point in our relationship had I ever spoken to her in that way...not in India and not before she left Ben. I never sought to manipulate her, but now I was. I knew that my life...and Samantha as my wife...were on the line.

"I'm not going back to Laura. You have to know that. I'm committed to you, and I'll wait as long as it takes. I love you." I was done passionately pleading with her.

"David, I love you, too. Please know I'm not leaving you for Ben. I'm leaving you for my kids. I can't stand to be without my kids fifty percent of the time. I hope that God will somehow help me forget you and the way you make me feel. I'm so sorry. I love you so much."

That was it. She closed her eyes one final time. I walked back into Kirk's house...dejected, crushed, and hopeless.

Earlier Kirk had called Ron Latimore to join us, because he thought that might help. We all met back at the hotel, and Ron arrived with a six-pack of beer to soothe my soul. What he didn't know is that I had never tasted beer in my life, and that night wasn't going to be the first. It was sort of a fundamentalist badge of honor to whip out from time to time...even though I had enjoyed other alcoholic drinks. I somehow felt proud to be a beer-virgin.

With my clothes still on, I crawled under the sheets, and I just laid there. I wanted to go to sleep and have the world completely fade away. Kirk, Dyno, and Ron enjoyed a few beers and watched a game while I curled up in a fetal position and closed my eyes. They had done all they could do.

Ron went home that night, and Dyno slept in the room next door to avoid Kirk's incessant snoring. All those f-bombs had worn me out so much that I never even heard him.

Friday, April 18th, 2008
The next morning, I woke up a little after 6am, and the world had not

faded away. Everything was still there, but I didn't want to be. Rather than laying there in the darkness waiting for Kirk to wake up, I decided to go workout in the hotel gym. I slipped on a shirt, shorts, and my running shoes, and I quietly closed the door behind me.

I made my way down to the gym and stepped on to the treadmill. "Maybe if I run fast enough I can get away from all of this," I thought to myself. I knew it wasn't true, but I was willing to resort to anything to trick my brain at this point.

The more I ran…the more I realized that my life was over. I had been willing to throw away everything I had worked for to be with Samantha, and now she was gone. Why should I even continue with my life? Why do I even need to live?

For the first time, I started contemplating suicide. What would it be like to jump off the top of the hotel? Or, maybe I could gulp down a bottle of pills. Neither seemed like plausible answers at that point, because I didn't want to end up paralyzed or just really sick…without actually killing myself.

So, I kept running.

By 7:30, I thought Kirk might be awake so I headed back to the room. As I walked in, he exhaled a sigh of relief.

"Duuuude! I'm glad to see you're okay. I woke up, and you weren't here and I thought…"

"You thought what?" I asked.

"Ya know…like you ended it."

"Nah. I thought about it this morning though."

"How ya doin'?" he asked.

"Not good...*really* not good."

As he clicked on the TV, I sat down on the chair next to my bed. I reached into my bag to pull out my laptop, and I opened it up to see if Samantha had emailed me.

My hopes were dashed...there was *nothing*.

I had to get in contact with her *somehow*. I just had to express my love, so I got the idea to send her flowers. After browsing online for a few moments, I decided to send Samantha 12 red roses and an "I love you!" balloon on Saturday and 24 red roses, six balloons, and a white stuffed bear on Monday...since they don't deliver on Sunday. I knew it was probably a bad idea to send all that stuff to her house, but I just *had* to be in contact somehow.

By this time, Dyno had made his way over from next door, and we were just hanging in the room. He has this uncanny way of asking a question that penetrates beyond the surface. I'm not sure what it is about him, but it's like he sees through you in this mystical sort of way.

"So...how's it goin' this morning?" he asked.

"Not good."

"What does 'not good' mean?"

That's when I could feel it coming. I could feel a welling up of the sadness that I had been pushing down with anger.

"I'm...just." My lips began to quiver, and my hands started to shake. My eyes squeezed tightly shut trying to hold it all back, and then it happened. There was a gush of emotion and tears that had been waiting to come out.

"I'm...just...not...sure...how I...can...go...on!"

It must have taken me five minutes to get that one sentence out between the sobs. I felt an utter darkness sweep over me that I didn't know how to stave off.

"Please don't leave me alone. I can't be alone today." I was begging them. I knew deep down inside that I wasn't in a good place, and I needed help.

They both did their best to comfort me, and I worked hard to suck it all back inside. We packed up our stuff and headed out for some breakfast. The question of the morning was, "What do we do to stay busy?" In their heads, Dyno and Kirk must have been thinking, "How the hell do we keep Dave from killing himself today?"

The answer, of course..."The Forbidden Kingdom"...a Jackie Chan flick at a popular theatre in Newport Beach.

On the way to the movie, I put a call in to Randy, my therapist, to alert him to the fact that Samantha had left. I needed to hear his words of wisdom, but he was out of town in Santa Barbara and all I got was his voicemail. After getting my butter-drenched popcorn, I found the guys already seated inside...right in the middle of the completely empty, mid-morning Friday movie.

Although I was mildly distracted during the previews, my mind was fully immersed in my loss of Samantha by the time Jackie Chan started chopping Chinese guys in half. I was so broken inside and desperate for some sense of relief when I finally felt my phone buzzing in my pocket.

My heart leapt with anticipation...hoping to see Samantha's number on the screen. Instead, it was a voicemail. I slipped out of the empty theatre to check to see if it was a message from her that had popped up without me receiving a call. Actually, it was my therapist...

> *"Hi David, this is Randy. I was just calling to check in on you. I'm here in Santa Barbara, and the reception isn't too good. I'm so sorry to hear about what has happened, and I'm anxious to speak*

with you. Give me a call back."

"How could I have missed his call? It didn't even ring," I said to myself.

I dialed his number. Voicemail.
I desperately dialed it again.
No answer…voicemail.

That's when it happened again. I could feel the rush of emotion flooding to the surface, and I couldn't hold it back. It was more powerful than my own willpower.

I burst out sobbing in front of the theatre, and I couldn't stop. It wasn't the "I'm-getting-a-bit-emotional-in-church" sort of cry. This was "I'm-at-the-Middle-East-wailing-wall" sobbing.

I felt so out of sorts that I just had to get to a place of comfort. After two months of feeling so abnormal, I needed something that felt somewhat normal again.

I just wanted to sit in my *car.*

For some reason, my white Ford Focus was the only thing in my mind that felt like "normal" to me, but it was over 25 miles away back at the apartment. Frankly, I didn't care, and I started walking.

I sobbed, and I walked.
I didn't tell Kirk or Dyno that I was leaving.
I just left. I had to get back to my car.

With tears streaming down my face and snot hanging down from my nose, I sobbed my way to Jamboree Road. As passing motorists stared at my sorry state, I started looking for a tall building to jump off of. Nothing seemed to suffice in my mind, so I kept walking toward my car.

My phone rang in my pocket, and it was Ron.

"Trotter, how ya feelin' today?" he asked in his usual upbeat tone.

"I can't handle it anymore. I can't handle it anymore." I just kept sobbing as I walked.

"Where are you at?" He sounded seriously concerned.

"I'm just walking," I said in an undecipherable voice masked by sobs. He finally pegged me down that I was on Jamboree after leaving the movie, and he immediately hung up to call Kirk and Dyno. Within five minutes, they pulled up beside me and tried to coax me into the car. I wouldn't have anything to do with it.

I just kept crying and saying, "I've got to get to my car, and I'm walking there."

"Dave, just get in the car, and we'll drive you to Cypress."

"No, I'm walking, and you can't *stop* me. I'm walking there. I *like* to walk."

Kirk jumped out of Dyno's car, and he started walking with me. We walked all the way down Jamboree together and turned right on Pacific Coast Highway. My sobbing had subsided, and Kirk and I were actually able to carry on a conversation as we walked. They kept trying to get me in the car, but I would have nothing to do with it.

There has always been something about walking that cleared my head, and my head definitely needed to be cleared more than ever.

While Dyno kept pace with his vehicle, I heard someone come running up from behind. It was Ron. When Ron heard about the mission, he joined us with his Subway sandwich in hand. Through both laughter and tears, the three of us walked and talked our way all the way down Pacific Coast Highway.

As we were approaching Hoag Hospital, where both of my children were born, I finally got a call from my therapist on Kirk's phone. I guess they had been in touch with him, and they were arranging a phone conversation with me.

"David, you *really* need to get some help today. I think it would be best if we got you in to see somebody."

"I'm okay, Randy. I just need to get to my car."

"I understand that, David, but I think you need *more* than that. The guys mentioned that you're near Hoag, and I think you should walk in to get some help."

The tears started to flow again. It was like a spout of sadness that I couldn't turn off. "No, I don't need to do that. A hospital is for *weak* people, and I can handle this. If I go in there, they may keep me, and I don't want that either."

I was scared to death that if I walked in to that hospital in a state of depression, they may never let me leave. Frankly, I was going to fight anyone and everyone that would try to get me into a mental hospital.

I hung up with Randy, and we kept walking.

With the cool, ocean breeze blowing on my face and friends to join me, this whole "walk-to-my-car" thing was working out quite well. After stopping for a Diet Coke at a convenience store on the way, we were almost ready to cross over into Huntington Beach,

With the city sign in sight, I could feel Kirk and Ron peeling back a bit. Time began to slow down as I turned and looked behind me to see a large, unmarked SUV and three police cars pull up to the curb.

"You *bastards*," I muttered at them as I saw my two friends standing off to the side with their heads down.

The policeman walked up and said, "Mr. Trotter, how ya doin' today?"

"Just fine...out for a little walk," I mumbled.

"Put your hands behind your back and step against the wall please. Do you have any weapons or sharp objects in your pockets?"

He proceeded to pat me down and check my pockets as my face pressed against the wall. "Go ahead and sit down on the curb for me."

The humiliation of being frisked on the side of PCH in Newport Beach as my two friends stood by was adding insult to injury.

"Mr. Trotter, are you planning to hurt yourself today?"

Having been a pastor for 10 years and dealt with a few situations of this sort, I knew all the right answers to give.

"Absolutely not," I parroted even though I had told Kirk otherwise earlier that morning.

"Are you sure about that? We're just here to help."

I proceeded to be an ass to all of the police officers including one who was a friend from back in the day at ROCKharbor Church. I didn't care. I was desperate to stay out of a hospital and get inside my white Ford Focus back in Cypress.

As they ran my driver's license and chatted with one another about what to do, Ron sat down next to me on the curb. The humiliation of sitting on a curb between two police cars on the side of PCH was agonizing.

"Bro, this is the *worst*. I can't believe you guys," I complained to Ron.

"Dave, we're just trying to help you. If you're not in a place to help yourself, sometimes it requires some outside support. Randy instructed us to do this, and we just want the best for you."

"The only thing good about sitting on this curb right now in Newport

Beach is the fact that everyone who drives by is thinking that the white guy is consoling the black guy for getting arrested," I joked in an effort to make light of the situation.

"That is *so* true!" he laughed.

We both cracked up at the situation, and it helped relieve the stress. After I told my whole story to the police, they dispatched a psychiatrist from the local department to come down and interview me. I knew what I had to say in order to avoid being locked up.

"No sir. I'm not going to hurt myself. I'm just a little depressed, and I think I need some rest."

That did it. After a lengthy interrogation to see if I was hearing demonic voices and what color my last stool was, I was released. Upon the recommendation of a friend, we headed over to a local urgent care to get some meds to shut down my brain.

After walking all that way, I was finally willing to get back in the car to drive there. The cordial doctor prescribed me some anti-anxiety pills, and I was feeling doped-up within an hour. Thank God something finally took away the feeling of wanting to crawl out of my skin.

Meanwhile, Ron called his wife, Rachel, for her creative support. While Kirk and I were having dinner, Ron and Rachel cleared out the apartment of anything that was connected with Samantha...things that she inadvertently left behind and things she had purchased for us. They completely re-arranged the living room and bedroom, and they brought over new artwork, dishes, and toys for my kids.

When Kirk and I walked in the door, they were there to greet me, and I was so grateful for their willingness to create a new "home" for me. Unfortunately, it still didn't take away the pain of being alone. That night, I sat down to write Samantha one last email...

My best friend, soul mate, lover, and wife,

Because of the intense pain I'm experiencing, my friends were gracious enough to clear out everything that belongs to you from our apartment and re-arrange it.

All of your remaining items (kids' stuff, movies, and games) and all items that you purchased (all food, cleaning supplies, my ring, dishes, silverware, sheets, bedspread, folding table, tablecloths, shower head, etc.) are in the possession of Ron Latimore. If your kids want their fish, just let Ron know, and he'll arrange to get them to you as well. If there is anything that I didn't give you that you'd like, please let me know.

I will keep the ring and necklace that I hope to give to you once again in the near future. They were intended for you and no one else as an intimate expression of my love. I love you, and I'm waiting for you.

Please visit my blog and remember the beauty of our relationship. You are the love of my life, and the only one for me.

David

I proceeded to upload all the photos of her and I together as well as photos of the kids onto my website. I wanted her to remember the great times that she was leaving behind. As I crawled into bed, Kirk ended up spending the night with me by sleeping on the living room couch.

Saturday, April 19th, 2008
Once again, I woke up before Kirk, and I headed out for a morning workout…except this time it was at my own gym. With my iPod blaring in my ears, I pushed and pulled for miles on the elliptical machine as I stared blankly into the muted televisions.

After thoroughly exhausting myself, I stopped by the store to pick up a number of the items that had been thrown out because they were purchased by Samantha. With bags in my hands, I ascended the stairs one by one back up to the front door of the apartment. Not "the" apartment... "our" apartment. No matter how many items I removed and replaced, it would always be ours.

We picked it out together.
We furnished it together.
We spent every day there together.
It was *ours*.

Kirk was just waking up, and I placed all the bags on the kitchen counter. Through his groggy eyes, he asked, "Have a good workout?"

"Yeah, it felt good to sweat it out, and I stopped by the store to replace a bunch of this stuff."

"How are you feeling about things this morning?"

The dam broke again. All it took was a single question, and I felt myself crumble inside. As I started to cry, my face contorted in agony. I leaned onto the counter to try to catch my breath. As Kirk walked toward me, my legs buckled underneath, and I hit the kitchen linoleum floor with a thud.

Through my sobs, I begged Kirk, "Take me somewhere. I need help today. I need help. I can't go on."

I was an utter mess, and I was finally ready to get some help...or so I thought. Later that morning, we toured a mental health facility that scared the hell out of me. The intake person even commented that I seemed to be too "high-functioning" to be there. We ended up leaving that place, and I somehow felt like I was back in a state where I could function on my own. After discussing my plans for the rest of the weekend, Kirk went back to be with his family that afternoon.

As I laid alone that night, I looked over on Samantha's side of the bed, and I longed to hold her in my arms. The woman I had given up everything in my life for was now gone. I looked through photos of us hiking through Azusa Canyon and our children playing together during the prior week. I reflected on the previous Friday when we exchanged rings and vows during our getaway, and I just hoped and prayed that she'd come back sometime soon.

Sunday, April 20th, 2008
Sundays were weird now that I wasn't leading Revolution anymore. Instead of waking up full of adrenaline to put on the Sunday show, I woke up wondering what the day had in store.

On this day, I had previously arranged to take Emerson, my five year old, to Disneyland in the morning and Waverly, my nine year old, to a father-daughter event that evening. I was disappointed that I couldn't hang out with them together, but I felt fortunate to see them at all since my life had fallen apart a few days earlier.

As I picked up Emerson from home around 8:30 in the morning, Laura informed me that his Disneyland pass was in the possession of our friends Jason and Jamie who lived nearby. A rush of anger shot through my body, and I wasn't looking forward to seeing them.

Someone had recently informed me how offended and angry Jamie was because I used a portrait she had taken of me for the new startarevolution.tv website. As a wedding photographer, she felt like she should have been asked beforehand...I guess. What I thought was once a close friendship had dwindled down to an offense over a mere photo.

I left Emerson in the car.
Knock, knock, knock.

"Laura said that you guys have the kids' Disneyland passes, and I just wanted to pick them up."

"Yeah, here ya go." Jamie handed them to me...faking sincerity.

As I began to walk away, I turned back toward her and an eruption of anger came from deep within. "Ya know, if you had a problem with me using the photo, you could have just contacted me directly rather than spreading how angry you are. *Fuck you*, Jamie, *fuck you!*"

With a surprised look on her face, she herded her two, pre-school kids inside the house, and I hopped back in the car with Emerson. As I sped away, tears began to flow down my face, and I knew that I *really* needed help now. I knew that I was in no condition to hang out with my son, and I needed to drop him back off as soon as possible.

By this time, Laura was already at church, and I tried to get a hold of her on her cell phone. Unfortunately, she didn't answer. I called the Director of Children's Ministry instead, and she picked up right away.

"I can't get a hold of Laura, and I need to drop Emerson off at church. I'm not in any condition to hang out with him. I need to go to the hospital."

"Okay, not a problem, bring him by the back entrance," she calmly responded.

As my mind spun out of control, I ensured that no one else would be with her as I transferred Emerson…every word accented with profanity. This wasn't just *any* church…this was *my* church. My worst nightmare would have been the people who I had invested so much time and energy with coming out from the service and harassing me just like they had online and via email. I was literally out of my mind, and I couldn't get to the hospital soon enough.

She took Emerson by the hand, and I immediately called Kirk to meet me at Fairview Hospital in Costa Mesa. Before I got onto the freeway, I knew there were several things I *had* to do…stop by the apartment to pack a bag, take down the photos from my blog, and say "good-bye" to Samantha.

As I pulled up to her house, neither car was in the driveway. I couldn't imagine her showing up to Revolution Church just a couple of days after returning home, so I hoped she was inside.

I knocked on the door, but there was no answer. I peered in the front window to see if I saw any signs of her presence. I walked back out to the front sidewalk and started calling her name, "Samantha! Samantha! I just want to say good-bye!"

No answer.

I went up to the garage door and looked through the window, but I couldn't see anything. Then, I walked over to the trash cans sitting to the left of the garage to see if they were there...the roses that is. They *were*...Saturday's delivery of roses with the card and balloon were ransacked and sitting on top of the trash.

My heart had been ransacked as well.

I got back in my car, and I drove straight to the hospital. Unfortunately, they were out of beds, so they arranged for a spot at Laguna Beach Medical Center a few miles away. Because I had verbalized thoughts of suicide, they couldn't let Kirk transport me, so they called an ambulance.

Two hours since my initial arrival, I was starting to mellow out and feel a bit back to normal. Having just finished lunch in the cafeteria with Kirk, the ambulance arrived. They strapped me on a gurney, and Kirk snapped a quick shot of me with his camera-phone as I was loaded inside.

I was back in my "right mind" for the moment, but I knew I still needed help.

Three Days in a Place Like No Other

After slapping down the $3,500 deposit on my credit card because they couldn't verify my insurance on a Sunday, I handed over my belongings, and they were searched and catalogued one by one. I hugged Kirk good-bye, and I was led through the double security doors to my room where I was encouraged to go to sleep since it was getting close to "lights out."

I took the pills they put in my hand, and I just wanted to close my eyes and make the world go away. I was scared to death to sleep in a place with a bunch of crazies…and then I realized that I might be one as well.

With the sun shining brightly into my room, I woke up the next morning to discover a beautiful ocean view and my roommate for the stay…a medical doctor who had spun out like me. It turned out that half of the 30 or so people in there were professionals of some sort…people that just pushed themselves too far or made some bad choices. The other half of the people…well, they're probably *still* there.

I made my way down the whitewashed hallway to the dining room. It was a square room with a kitchen counter and sink on one end and long tables throughout. Patients chose from a menu that was presented each morning, but I was given a standard breakfast of eggs, toast, fruit, and juice since I had not placed an order the day before. It was hospital food, but it was edible.

Less than 20 of us were gathered around a set of tables that morning, and people were quiet and kept to themselves. There were a few talkative ones in the bunch who complained about the food or the shortness of the shower. I kept my head down, but people couldn't help but notice the 6' 5" new guy.

"What's your name?"

"David."

"Welcome…good to have you."

"Thanks…I guess."

People kept eating, but there is a natural inquisitiveness in everyone's mind that asks, "What are you in for?" as if we were in prison. In some sense, we were. I couldn't get out if I wanted to even though I had checked myself in. Others were given a free stay without asking…if you know what I mean.

Conversation eventually came around to my side of the room, and some-one had the nerve to say, "So...why are *you* here?"

Rather than make up a story about hearing voices or seeing dead people, I just told the truth. I was a pastor who left my wife for another wom-an...and she left me.

"Ohhhhhh..."

You could hear a synchronized moan spread through the room. Yes, I was one of *those* guys. I kept eating, and people mostly left me alone.

After scraping my tray and placing it on the metal cart, I walked back down to my room...looking along the way to get a visual lay of the land. Some people were lying in bed curled up in a ball. Others were reading or looking out the window. And, some...they were walking the halls mumbling to themselves as their heads swung back and forth.

During shower time, I was given permission to shave under supervision, and it felt refreshing to get cleaned up and put on a new set of clothes. With no shoes in our possession, everyone was walking around in bare or socked feet. It felt like a slumber party for people who were out of their minds.

My first day included meeting with a psychiatrist to continue my anti-anxiety meds and start on anti-depressants as well. After he diagnosed me with "major depression," I was encouraged to attend group sessions and get plenty of sleep. I opted out of the sessions, since the people freaked me out, and I really didn't want to hear about someone else's problems when mine seemed overwhelming enough.

I slept, I ate, and I exercised in my room.
I tried to just forget about everything that had happened.
And...I called Laura.

"Hi Laura..." my voice sounded strange to myself.

"Are you okay?" she asked.

"Not really, she left me." I can't believe I was calling her, but I was so desperate for someone...anyone...to listen.

I told her the story of sensing that something was wrong on Thursday morning and how I was devastated by the disconnected phone. I rehashed walking into the apartment to find Samantha's note and the place empty, and I poured out my heart about how much pain and agony I was in.

"David, this is really awkward for me to listen to."

"*What?* What are you talking about? I'm dying in here...can't you understand that?"

I didn't understand why she couldn't simply listen, and I eventually just hung up.

By day two, I began to get the hang of the place, and I felt comfortable enough to attend a group session. We gathered in a smaller room and circled up our chairs. As the staff member facilitated the discussion, most people stayed on target, but there was one guy who kept interrupting like a four year old. They finally had to remove him so that we can actually function as a group.

The facilitator talked all about crises and how we tend to deal with them...the difference between an emergency and something that's become a pattern in our lives. "Yada, yada, yada" is all I heard. I was dying inside and all this analysis was going nowhere in my brain.

She asked us to grab a sheet of paper and make three columns for a self-inventory...physical, psychological, and social. "Give yourself a number from one to 10 based on how you feel like you're doing in each area," she said.

Physical – 9
Psychological – 2
Social – 5

Physically, I had been working out and feeling stronger. Psychologically, I was about ready to end everything. Socially, I had three friends and a therapist who were willing to walk with me...that's all.

After she told us to "be nice to yourself," I made a list of goals for the day. That was my way of being nice, because I liked meeting goals more than anything else. I wrote...

1. Attend all groups.
2. Call my three friends.
3. Avoid obsessing and re-focus my attention.
4. Work out.
5. Read.

I went back to my room, and I did pretty good on my goals for the day, but I did keep obsessing. I couldn't help but think of how much pain I was in. I wrote in two-inch tall scribbled writing...

I'm in so much grief and pain. I left everything. I gave her everything. She left me. Samantha can't handle being with a man like me! I will not be alone now that Samantha is not in my life.

I just kept writing out everything that came to me so that I could get it out of my head...

I'm in a psych hospital. Samantha is at home – happy and with Ben. I'm fucking miserable. I'm dying inside. I hate people who are stupid. Samantha crushed my heart. Samantha is killing me. Samantha betrayed me and deceived me. The pain is so intense that I just can't handle it. God is nothing more than content for a show. My first wife is so fucking angry, and it hurts. I have so few reasons left to live. I'd love to find someone who will truly love me, care for me, and be intimate with me. I left everything. I gave Sa-

*mantha everything I have, had, or will have. I have nothing left. I
miss Samantha tremendously. I'm jealous of her new found family,
freedom, and happiness. When I see her body or face, I'm in pain.
I have no one to go home to again (not Samantha and not Laura).*

Ahhh…I got it all out. My stream of consciousness sounded so disgust-
ing to my own ears, but I had to get it out of me. The meds were making me tired, so I crawled into bed and fell asleep until lunchtime. The
afternoon was filled with a group session, some reading, a workout, and
a meeting with the chaplain.

I was finally starting to feel better about things, and I knew that I had to
focus on the positive if I was going to make it through. On another sheet
of paper, I wrote…

*I am becoming physically, emotionally, and spiritually strong.
I am focusing on me, my health, and my future.
I am living my life and no one else's life.
I am a lover of people.
I am not alone.
I will find and marry an amazing, passionate, connecting, inti-
mate, woman.
I will use my gifts and talents to make a significant income to ben-
efit myself and others.
I will share my story for the benefit of the world.*

Every time I talked with Kirk, I kept asking for big sheets of white paper…the kind that hangs on a flip chart…the kind I used to brainstorm
with at Revolution. Because of weird schedules, Kirk, Ron, and Dyno
weren't able to come by, but one of their friends named Tim Timmons
finally brought the paper.

Back in the day, Tim was a well-known pastor in Orange County who
led a mega-church, and he had experienced his fair share of pain over
the years. He sat and listened patiently…hearing all about my love for
Samantha and the meltdown that ensued after I left Laura and resigned
from Revolution. As soon as he walked out the door, I unrolled the large

sheets of paper and hung them on the stark white walls of my bedroom. My roommate had gone home by now, so I was left to decorate any way that I pleased.

On one piece of paper, I wrote "Old Life" at the top…on the other "New Life." I wanted to clearly articulate the things about my old life that I didn't want anymore, and I wanted to set my eyes on the things in a new life that I could be intentional about getting.

OLD LIFE	NEW LIFE
Consumed by ministry	Connected to God
Driven workaholic	Passionate (able to turn it on/off)
Disconnected marriage (obligation)	Interested in an intimate marriage
Disconnected from kids (obligation)	Strong connection with kids
Fearful of other's opinions and expectations	Freedom to live my life with God
Identity = success and marriage	Identity = internal world
Samantha was a parachute / escape.	No need to escape (ego strength, coping skills, and support system)
Isolate from what's uncomfortable	Move toward them with courage
High need to control outcomes	Do my part and trust God with the rest
Utilitarian relationships	True friends, peers, clients, and biz associates
My pain & anger toward Revolution's response	Grace, forgiveness, and repentance
Motivate others toward my goals	Motivate others toward their goals
Fearful of creativity because of conformity or frivolity	Creativity for fun, playfulness, expression, and financial success.

I worked on those two lists for several hours with brutal honesty and a struggle to envision the new life that I truly wanted.

In the midst of it all, I had a mental picture of me driving a black Mercedes Benz down Pacific Coast Highway with a beautiful blonde woman in the passenger seat. I couldn't make out her face, but I saw the wind blowing through our hair and huge smiles on our faces.

The moment wasn't necessarily a symbol of "success"…more symbolic of a freedom to enjoy life and experience intimacy. As I was growing up, we owned Fords and Chevrolets and practical cars that didn't have electric doors or windows…"cause that stuff might break." We were more of a practical family that didn't value self-expression as much as doing what was reasonable. Buying a Mercedes was definitely not practical nor reasonable based on my upbringing.

Somehow the vision forced its way into my heart, but I could barely imagine myself in this situation intellectually. I was in more debt than ever, and I doubted that any woman (much less a hot blonde) would want to be with me anytime soon.

After I was done with my two lists, I made another list of 20 affirmations for myself…holding on to the great things that God had put inside of me.

The funny thing is that I didn't necessarily feel that close to God while I was in this dark place. Usually, during difficult times in my life, I'd sense a Divine Presence that was re-assuring. Ironically, I felt that Presence strongly while I was with Samantha, but I felt alone as I struggled to figure out a new life while I was locked inside.

I had to trust that God was still with me though. Through all my seminary training and reading of the Bible, I knew the truth that God wouldn't leave me alone in my time of darkness. Even if I couldn't feel it…I trusted that to be the case.

By Wednesday afternoon, I was impatient to check out, and thankfully… the hospital staff felt like I was ready. After meeting with the psychiatrist about my follow-up plan for meds, therapy, a brain scan, and relational support, I was discharged.

I was a free man.
With practically nowhere to go.

DEALING WITH DESTRUCTION

After spending three days pumped full of meds in a white-walled hospital, I felt like the world had a fogginess to it as I stepped outside once again. My black-PCH-walking-partner Ron pulled up, and I tossed my bag into his backseat. He flashed his effusive bright smile exuding energy, and he embraced me with both arms.

"Great to see you, Trot-ee-ay!" He loves to call me by my last name with his own added flair as if I'm royalty or something.

"Whaaat's uuup brooo?" I said in slow motion. Everything seemed a little sluggish at that point. "Feels good to be back in the normal world again."

"Yeah, I bet…where ya wanna go?"

"I don't know. I should probably just head back to the apartment…figure out what to do next."

Despite my mental haze, I was already starting to develop a plan to get out of that place. I knew I couldn't stay there. It was just too painful to live in an environment that Samantha and I had made as our home.

Even though I was well aware that I'd be walking back in to find the couch in a new location and the bed set at a new angle thanks to Ron and Rachel, nothing could take away the memories of Samantha and I enjoying life together in that space. I knew that I *had* to get out.

While I stared off into the traffic along the 405 freeway, Ron was full of excitement.

"Trot-ee-ay, this is a *great* day. Today is the day I'd buy stock in you if I could."

"Huh?" I wasn't catching on.

"That's right. If somebody was selling stock in Dave Trotter, I'd be leveraging everything to put my money on you today."

"What do you mean?"

"I *mean* that you're at the bottom, but you're gonna to rise to the top. That's when you buy stock…when no one else wants it…when it's hit the low point."

"Thanks…I think."

"Duuude! My money's on you! Before you know it, you'll be more successful than you ever were in the past. Listen to what I'm sayin'."

I didn't know what to think. It sounded like a "your-friend-just-got-out-of-the-mental-hospital" speech written for the ride home. I wasn't really buying into it, but if he was, I was fine with that. I needed people to believe in me, because I wasn't sure I believed in myself.

Since Ron and Rachel were leaving in a couple of days for vacation, they invited me to house and dog sit for them over the weekend. That meant I only had to spend two nights in the apartment by myself. Even though they offered for me to stay at their place during those first two nights, I just felt like I would be intruding into their lives more than I already had.

Heading to Court

After arriving back at the apartment, I pulled out my cell phone to check for any voicemails. It turns out that my divorce attorney had been trying to get a hold of me for the last two days to share the good news.

My wife was taking me to court to gain temporary custody of the kids, because I had freaked out in front of Emerson on the day I checked myself in to the hospital.

"May I speak with Scott Jarvis, please?"

"Yes, one moment," the receptionist said.

"This is Scott Jarvis. May I help you?"

"Scott, it's David Trotter. You've been trying to get a hold of me?"

"*Yeah,* where have you been?"

"Uh...I've...I've been in the hospital for three days."

"We have to know these things. You need to keep us informed about anything that would affect your case."

Seriously? This guy is *scolding* me for not calling him while I'm in a psych hospital. He's obviously never been through the hell I have.

It turned out that we had a court appointment on Friday where the judge could give my wife full, temporary custody of the kids. My attorney's plan was to work toward an agreement outside of the courtroom.

Friday arrived, and I slipped on my dress slacks that were now hanging off me like my big brother's clothes. The "affair and divorce diet" was really working now.

I walked into the giant hallway of the county courthouse to see my wife and two of our friends sitting with her on a bench. One gal was the Children's Director at Revolution, and the other gal was a fellow staff member back in the day at ROCKharbor Church. As Laura looked away, I stared at all three of them with vengeance in my heart.

Although I was glad that Laura had their support, it also felt like I was left all alone to fend for myself. I headed straight toward my one ally, my attorney, for last minute preparations.

"David, I've already spoken with your wife's attorney, and I think we can come to an agreement outside the court room. How do you feel about..." He was interrupted by the presence of my wife's attorney as she walked up.

"Have you explained the options to your client yet?" she butted in.

"We were just getting ready to go over those now," he responded kindly.

"Well, he needs to know that..." She continued on until I was sick of listening.

"Get this lady out of here." I said it right in front of her...I didn't care. "I don't have to listen to this *crap*. She's not my attorney."

He shooed her away, and we discussed my option. There weren't really *options* on the table. There was one option.

Either I get to see the kids three times a week for three hours each time with a chaperone…or she planned to go into the courtroom and fight for temporary custody.

I opted for three times a week, and we arranged for three of our friends to be the chaperones by making a few calls on the spot. The utter humiliation of being followed around by a personal friend while I spend time with my own children would be worth it. I didn't care. I just wanted to salvage my relationship with the two most precious people on the planet.

Hangin' With Louie
That night, I sucked it up and slept at the apartment alone…trying to focus on anything other than the fact that my second "wife" left me and I spent three days in a psych ward with a bunch of loonies.

After a couple of cloudy days of survival, I packed a quick bag for the weekend, and I drove down to Costa Mesa to hang at the Latimore's home. They told me where I could find a spare key right inside the door of the garage. As I walked up their front sidewalk, I opened the side door, and I felt around on the wall for a light switch. As my eyes adjusted to the lone bulb shining into the darkness of the overstuffed garage, I looked in front of me to see several boxes of stuff from my apartment… the bedspread off Samantha's bed, the flip flops she bought me, her kids' movies, and the dishes we had purchased together.

I grimaced, and I grabbed the key to get out of there as soon as I could. I flipped off the switch and left everything in the darkness behind.

After letting myself in, I headed straight to the back door to let in their dog named Louie, a giant white Wheaten Terrier. With his front legs prancing around their wooden kitchen floor, Louie and I got more acquainted with one another. He obviously remembered me from our initial meeting when Samantha and I had gone over for dinner one night.

I scratched behind his ears as we took stock of one another...him wagging his huge tongue and me wondering what the weekend would hold.

Later that night, I sprawled out on the couch in their living room, and Louie curled up on the area rug right next to me. With Letterman's monologue turned up just loud enough to drown out the suicidal thoughts in my head, I closed my eyes and hoped that sleep would somehow wash away the pain.

The next morning, the pain was still there...but so was Louie. With nothing else on the agenda, I decided that a run on the beach would be good for both of us. We loaded into the Focus and made our way down to Newport Beach for an early morning run. Ron said that Louie liked to go to the beach, but within a half a mile, he was having a hard time keeping up. We walked the rest of the way...and I found out later on that Louie has hip dysplasia. That would have been good to know before I dragged him for over a mile.

Although I appreciated the constant human connection of the guys before I spent time in the hospital, there was something strangely comforting about the companionship of Louie over the weekend. I wouldn't necessarily call myself an 'animal lover' although I did grow up with a cat or dog most of my life. There was something healing about sitting down on the couch while a giant furry friend put his head in my lap. No words needed to be exchanged. It was the simple warmth of man and dog together.

By Sunday, I was ready for a little human connection, and I decided to venture into a church that I had always heard about called Soul Survivor. They met in the space of a defunct sports store at an empty mall in the center of Costa Mesa. I parked across the street and made my way toward the crosswalk hoping not to see anyone I knew.

As I entered the space, I watched the awkward pre-service preparations that most small churches go through. Through the mic, guitar, and video projector checks, the pastor greeted people with a hug and signaled for the service to begin. With less than 50 people in attendance, it felt like a giant living room where everyone just happened to be facing the same direction. I could be wrong, but I think everyone knew one another, and I didn't know a soul…thankfully. I didn't feel like explaining my situation, and I enjoyed being incognito.

I *did* notice the gal who got up to give the sermon that day…the daughter of one of the board members who fired me for the paymystudentloan. com videos at that church six years back. Despite the fact that southern California is a huge place, it seems like I can never go anywhere without a connection to someone or something…in this case, a reminder of more pain.

Her style was casual and laid back with little effort exerted to impress any of us…kind of like the entire service. Frankly, it was driving me nuts! My mind was running wild with all the ways they could make the program better as I watched the somewhat chaotic, even haphazard, worship service. I was accustomed to leading services where practically every movement and moment was accounted for.

As the speaker continued to share her heart about the Scriptures for the day, my mind settled down, and I started to actually enjoy the simplicity of it all.

All in all, I just felt numb. I didn't sense a Divine Presence or Jesus or God or anything. It's not because God wasn't there. I'm sure He was… but I couldn't *feel* Him. I was so jumbled up inside about life, church, God, and ministry. Not much of it made sense to me. Frankly, I felt like I was just trying to survive each day. Thankfully, I could go home to Louie…he was there to keep me company.

Moving…Again

On Monday morning, I started searching for a new apartment. Although I didn't want to move farther away from my kids, I needed the support of Kirk and Ron if I was going to make it in this new life. Since they lived in Orange County, I started my search there…looking for an apartment that would take credit card for the deposit and monthly payment.

I found 'Coronado at Newport'...a huge complex in Newport Beach
with a newly renovated apartment that was calling my name...mainly
because it came with a plasma TV already mounted to the living room
wall.

I signed the lease, handed them my credit card, and called my new friend
John Weeks to help with the move. When I moved from my house in
Lakewood to the apartment in Cypress, I did it with the help of a day
laborer, and things were harder than I imagined. This time, I took John
up on his offer to use his company's work truck to pack it all up. It's
amazing what you can accumulate in 6 short weeks.

After hauling everything down the stairs into his behemoth truck, we
strategically positioned a number of items near the door that I would
be taking back over to the garage at my old house. They wouldn't fit in
the new apartment in Newport Beach, and Laura was willing to give me
some different pieces of furniture in exchange.

As the sun was setting and we rounded the corner to where my family
lived without me on Lemming Street, I noticed that our neighbors at the
end of the street were having a birthday party in their backyard. To see
them celebrating filled me with sadness as I was reminded of the loss of
love in my life. All I could hope for was that a move to Newport Beach
would be a fresh start.

As John and I unloaded the truck with Jim, one of John's friends, I noticed several people walking down the sidewalk toward my house. It
was our neighbor Louis (the one who alerted me that Samantha was
freakin' out in that Indian church) and a number of friends from Revolution who were at the party down the street. I walked out to the front
sidewalk to greet them.

"Hey guys. What's up?" I extended my hand to shake theirs, and they
recoiled and denied me.

"What's up..." they responded out of mere obligation.

I just turned around to get back to work while they stood at the front fence talking to one another. Yet, their attention would soon turn toward me.

"Hey Dave!" Louis yelled. "I heard your girlfriend broke up with you!" I looked up momentarily, but I decided to do the same thing that I had done for the past weeks...I ignored the taunting.

"How much did you have to pay that doctor to sign you out of the hospital? Huh?"

I shook my head in disbelief that the friend who I had introduced to Jesus and travelled with to India was now standing in front of my house with others from Revolution Church...mocking me.

"What's that guy's problem?" asked Jim, John's friend who was not a churchgoer in the least.

"I don't know Jim. They're just mad at me. Ignore them, and let's just get this done."

"I hope you feel a million times more pain than your wife and kids are going through right now!" my neighbor yelled over the fence.

I kept working and didn't even look at them or respond. They all finally walked away, but my heart was shattered. I knew that my actions were selfish and that I had hurt many people, but to come down to my house to harass me while I was unpacking...that was just low.

The next day, we unloaded the rest of the stuff at my new apartment, and I did my best to make the space my own. After purchasing a new area rug, bedspread, candles, and throw pillows, things were starting to shape up. There was something liberating about putting everything in place the way I wanted it to be...not needing to ask for someone else's opinion. Decorating the space was energizing, and I was experiencing the freedom that I longed for...just not with Samantha.

As I crawled in to bed that first night, my mind was consumed by thoughts of her laying next me. I laid there on the left side of the bed and stared over at her pillow. I longed to see her beautiful smile beaming back at me. I reached over to caress her face, but she was not there. My heart was aching for her presence, yet she was nowhere to be found. I tossed and turned and barely got a moment of sleep that night.

The next night was no different. I crawled in bed with the best of intentions to keep my mind off of her, but there was no use. She consumed my every thought.

Did she miss me?
Would she ever return?
What was she doing?

After a couple of nights of tossing and turning in the bed we purchased together, I couldn't handle it anymore. I pulled my pillow and my newly purchased comforter off the bed and headed toward the couch…popping a few sleeping pills along the way. Since it was taking two weeks to get cable installed, I watched rented movies until falling asleep after midnight as I curled up on the black, corduroy couch that left long lines all over my body and face. I woke up every morning looking like I had been run over by a set of Hot Wheels…and feeling like a Mack truck had hit me.

With nothing else to do, I kept working out at least once a day and sometimes even twice. I'd wake up each morning on the couch and slip on a pair of shorts and running shoes before walking over to the gym in my apartment complex. As I'd step on the elliptical machine, I'd turn on the morning news to catch up on the events of the world. The hour of cardio and lifting were a desperately needed distraction of adrenaline that took away the pain of it all. The pain relief was so helpful that I often found myself back in the gym at the end of the day as well.

No only was I working out daily, but I stopped eating fast food, too. Having grown up with McDonald's and Burger King as a regular part of my diet, I hit a drive thru once or twice a day for most of my adult life. I

started snacking on carrots and celery and eating a more healthy diet...
including protein drinks twice a day. Within three months of returning
from India, I lost of total of 35 pounds...down to a slim 180.

Two Sisters Reach Out...in Different Ways

Through all the emails and blog posts, one person's continual harass-
ment was ongoing and unwavering...Darlene Smallton, mother of Jamie,
the "get-my-damn-permission-before-you-use-my-photo" gal I freaked
out on the day I melted down. From the moment I left Laura and resigned from Revolution, Darlene had been sending a steady stream of
emails...at least four to five a week. Darlene attended Revolution from
time to time when her daughter or son-in-law were playing a part in a
holiday production, but I didn't see her very often other than that. She
somehow felt the freedom to speak into my life though.

She rebuked me by quoting scriptures from the Bible.
She bullied me with threats of what God would do.
She harassed me with words of 'advice.'
She even guilted me with stories of my children hanging out with her
grandchildren.

I finally blocked her email address so that I wouldn't have to see the
nonsense that was obviously flowing out of her own pain and anguish.

Ironically, her sister, Sharon, was one of the only people who reached
out to me after I got out of the hospital. She is a 50-something woman who is a passionate follower of Jesus who speaks at churches and
retreats regularly. Through an initial email, she indicated that she felt
compelled to send me some money as a gift, but she didn't want anyone
in her family to know that we'd been in contact. Through our back and
forth emails, she also offered to just sit in listen...without judgment...if
I was interested in sharing some of my experience.

I was thankful for the financial support, but I was leery about meeting
with her. Was this just a guise to bring more abuse that her sister Darlene was so skilled at doling out? Was this just a set up for some sort of
intervention?

I was so desperate for human contact that I agreed to meet with her at a coffee shop across the street from my apartment. I figured I could make a quick getaway if she got all crazy and started trying to cast demons out of me like Samantha did in India. As I walked up, I could feel myself begin to sweat with nervousness. Yet, the sight of her warm smile and quick embrace were a welcome experience in comparison to all the attacks I'd been getting from her sister.

"David, it is *great* to see you." I immediately felt her sincerity. "I want you to know that I work a lot with women who are going through divorce or have experienced broken marriages, and I'm anxious to learn from you. You can share as much or as little as you want…your story is yours to tell…it's safe with me."

"Sharon, I don't want anything I share to make it back to anyone in your family…okay?"

"Of course, I want this to be a safe place."

I never had more than a five minute conversation with this woman, but I poured out my heart to her on that day. Over the next hour, I told her my entire story…the whole thing…good, bad, and ugly. Burnout, exhaustion, connection in India, leaving, resigning, sex, and the hospital. All of it.

She stared at me intently and asked clarifying questions from time to time. Her frequent nods and verbal affirmations encouraged me to keep going as I bared my soul.

This was the first time I told my story to anyone other than my therapist and the guys who experienced it alongside me. I felt naked, and it was healing.

"Sharon, I'm not sure a woman will ever want to be with me again after the mess I've made."

"That's not true. As women, we want honesty and humility. Your transparency to me shows that you have both. You've got to be careful though. You don't need a half-glass woman. You need a full-glass woman who's sure of herself and has things together. Take your time, and God will bring someone."

"I guess...I know that it won't happen any time soon, but that's the whole reason why I did all this was to be find a partner in life. This is all so painful."

"I understand...what about Laura? What about getting back together with her?"

"I'm not interested. I'm not attracted to her any more, and I just don't have any feelings left."

"Not a chance?" she asked.

"Not a chance."

"So, what you're telling me is that if it was God's will for you to be with Laura, you wouldn't be open to it?"

She pulled the 'God card' on me...but she did it in a nice way.
She wasn't trying to bully me or manipulate me.
She was just genuinely interested in what God might want for my life.

"Well, I guess...if that's what He wanted...but I don't think it'll happen. We're done."

Restrained by the Law
Meanwhile, Ben had been in contact with Ron to pick up a few things that she inadvertently left behind...and to pass along my copy of the legal paperwork he filed for a restraining order against me.

Ben had hired an attorney to file the documents articulating their family's fear of me contacting them...making it sound like the relationship was one-sided with me pursuing Samantha. And, their neighbor said I was continuing to drive through the neighborhood.

"Great! This is just what I need…a needless restraining order. This is not going to help my cause to keep joint custody of my kids."

"I know Trot-ee-ay. I told him that I wished he would've talked to me before he did this. There's no need." Ron knew that I didn't have plans to contact her, and I had no intention of ever harassing their family at any point in time.

I immediately contacted my attorney by phone, but he passed along some bad news. Because he was also Samantha's divorce attorney, it was a conflict of interest for him to represent me. I'd either have to get another attorney or represent myself. Since I had to respond within three days, I didn't have the time or money to get another lawyer.

I was committed to beat this thing on my own…*no matter what.*

According to the paperwork and my research, I needed to prove why I was not a threat to their family. In my mind, the best way to prove that was through overwhelming evidence that our relationship was two-sided and that I was not interested in any further contact.

I spent eight hours typing up complete documentation of our relation-ship from beginning to end…connecting in India, kissing in Ben's car, and making love in San Diego…including photocopies of all my credit card purchases and her signature on our apartment lease. I included color photos of Samantha and I kissing as well as hanging out with all the kids…and a package of her birth control she left behind. I even got certified letters from the hospital psychiatrist and my therapist that I was no threat to their family.

There was *no possible way* I was going to get hit with a restraining or-der…and I didn't mind humiliating Ben in the process.

After I was done photocopying all the documentation, I headed down to the county office to hire the Sheriff to serve Ben the papers. That meant that he could be served at his office or at home...either way, he'd be looking at a stack of paperwork that he wouldn't want to read.

My hope was that they would drop the case or they'd go ahead and take it to court. I was hoping that he would be so humiliated by all the evidence that he wouldn't want to take it to a public setting. In my head, I was thinking, "Don't *fuck* with Dave Trotter. There's no need for a restraining order, but if you want to play that game, I'll win."

My adrenaline was pumping for days, and then I started to think twice about things. I wasn't sure that my hard-core tactics would be that helpful in my effort to have equal time with my kids in the end. Laura may not look very kindly on all this.

After several conversations with Kirk and Ron, they both encouraged me to be a class act in the situation and choose not to fight it. Once again, these guys were right. My desire for vengeance was unhelpful, and I needed to take immediate action in a different way.

Although Ben had already been served with the papers, I gave his attorney a call to discuss the matter.

"I just wanted to let you know that if you take this to court, I don't plan to fight the restraining order."

"Um...okay..." His attorney was obviously perplexed.

"What I'm saying is that the manner in which I responded to the paperwork is not the same way that I'll respond in court. I don't plan to have any contact with Samantha or their family, and I won't fight the restraining order if that's what happens."

The attorney was thoroughly confused, but I did my best to explain my change of heart in the matter.

Meanwhile, Samantha was struggling to get her name off the lease at our apartment in Cypress. I had to sign a document to agree to this change, but I refused to sign it. When she moved out, she left me with all the utility bills and the lease as well. My attorney suggested that I draft a list of the expenses, and he would approach her about splitting them 50/50. She refused to pay anything at all, and I wanted her to be on the hook for the remainder of the lease alongside me.

As things were unfolding, Ron's plan was to contact Ben directly and try to work things out on my behalf. Through multiple phone calls, he negotiated for me to have her name removed from the lease and a commitment that I'd never contact her or their family again…and Ron would personally guarantee it.

24 hours before the case was to go to court, I received a call from Ben's attorney. *They dropped everything.* I breathed a sigh of relief. I had her name removed from the lease, and the management company charged me instead…once again on my credit card.

The Consuming Darkness

All the while, the consuming darkness was growing more and more bleak. Although I was essentially non-functional during the three days before entering the hospital, now I felt like I had entered a cloud of depression after moving to Newport Beach. The loneliness of living by myself was all consuming.

After growing up in my parents' home for 18 years, I moved to college where I was surrounded by a roommate and other guys in the dorms. After my junior year, Laura and I got married, and we moved into the campus apartments together. For 35 years, I had lived with someone else, and now I was all alone. There was a long line of apartments that stretched to the right and left of mine, but I didn't know anyone…and no one seemed interested in knowing me.

I ate alone.
I slept alone.
I watched movies alone.

The funny thing is that I loved to be alone when I lived with my family. The noise of my kids drove me nuts, and I usually wanted to zone out in front of my computer or the TV. Better yet, I loved the solitude of going to a movie or shopping by myself. I loved my wife and kids, but I just didn't love being *with* them.

Now, I just wished I had someone to talk to. Not only had I never lived alone, but I hadn't really every been *single* either. I got married in college, and I pretty much bypassed any since of the single life at all. Now, I wondered what it was going to feel like to be on the dating scene as a 30-something.

As I was driving back from the beach one day, I heard a radio ad for a dating service called eHarmony. I had never even considered a service such as this, but now I was wondering what it would be like. After a quick perusal of the website, I whipped out my credit card and signed up for the $300 or so fee.

I filled out the online profile, and it said I'd be getting 'matches' within days. They weren't kidding. My inbox was flooded with over 10 matches every day of the week.

The truth is that I wasn't ever going to date any of these women. I wasn't going to lie about my situation, and I knew that no one was going to be interested in the *real* me. Seriously…who wants to date a guy who just left his wife of 15 years and is suffering through the pain of losing the woman he left his wife for?

Yeah, I was a prime catch for sure!

Frankly, I just wanted to 'try on' what it felt like to be single and searching for a partner. I wanted to send messages back and forth and get the feeling of it all…but it didn't really help much.

I was still all alone at night, and I desperately wanted to feel loved once again.

After calling Kirk, Ron, and Dyno so many times, I felt the awkwardness of my continual intrusion into their lives. None of them said anything, but I just started to feel like I was their personal leach...sucking
life out of them at any point I could.

I was dying for connection.
I was dying for love.
Frankly, I just wanted to die.

In fact, my thoughts of suicide were far worse after I got out of the hospital than before going in. I think the reality of my life began to set in
after all the initial trauma of Samantha leaving wore off. I was willing
to walk through the fire to be with her, but I wasn't planning to live this
life on my own...all alone.

From the moment I woke up until the moment my eyes finally closed as
I laid on the couch, my mind was clouded with thoughts of ending my
life. What was there to live for? I left Laura. Samantha was gone. My
career was destroyed. I was still getting harassing emails from people.

I just wanted to end the pain.
I wanted the darkness to go away.

I thought about swallowing all the sleeping pills in my bathroom medi-
cine cabinet. I pondered the thought of jumping from the top of the over-
pass along the 55 freeway. I even wondered how long it would take me
to purchase a gun from a pawn shop.

Yet, there was one thing that prevented me from crossing the line every
time...*my kids*.

I didn't want Waverly and Emerson to grow up with a legacy of suicide.
I didn't want them to be left with a giant hole in their life...a childhood
with no father. I just couldn't do that to them. Every time I thought of
ending my life, their faces would invade the darkness that consumed
me. The sweetness and beauty of their lives stopped me from carrying it
through. I was in so much agony, but I didn't want to cause them even

more pain than I already had.

Despite the presence of their faces, the darkness was becoming unbearable.

One Friday night, I was headed to a movie by myself when my mom called. Although I wasn't in contact with my dad at all, my mom and I had spoken a few times after I got out of the hospital. As I stood outside of a bookstore waiting to go into the movie, I poured out my heart to her.

"Mom, I'm *dying*. I feel like ending my life now more than ever. I just can't find that many reasons to live. I've walked away from so much, and I've lost whatever else I had left. I just don't know if I can take it any more."

I can't imagine hearing my own child say that and being powerless to change their situation, but that's the position my mom found herself in. She didn't try to over-mother me like she often would. Instead, she just listened, and that's what I needed. I needed to know that someone was with me and that they cared about me. Unfortunately, the darkness returned after the movie was over...as I walked back into my apartment and saw our bed once again.

I thought about dismantling the whole thing and shoving it in the trash, but I was just too cheap to do it. I paid good money for that bed and mattress, and I didn't want to throw it out. Yet, I didn't want to sleep on it either. Like I did every night, I grabbed a pillow and comforter and crawled onto the couch...watching late night TV until I was too exhausted to keep my eyes open any more.

The next morning after working out, I was overwhelmed by thoughts of Samantha as I sweated to the sound of music we listened to together. The music, the thoughts of her, the depression...it was becoming too much to handle. As I paced back in forth in front of the tennis courts, I began to cry uncontrollably. The tears streamed down my face, and my cry was audible to those coming and going from the gym. I had to talk with someone...I just *had* to.

I pulled my cell phone out of my pocket and called Kirk…hoping he was available to talk.

"Hello?"

"Kirk…hey…I need to talk…I'm dying." I was crying and sniffing so much that I'm surprised he could even understand me.

"What's going on?"

"I just can't take it any more. I'm in so much pain." My broken heart was manifesting in physical pain and an extreme tightness in my chest.

"What happened, Dave?"

"I don't know. I just…I just think I've got three options today. I think today may be the day…the day I just end it all."

I was serious about it. I was so sick and tired of life, and I just wanted it all to go away. I did have two more options in my head though.

"Or, I just have to suck it up and hope that a woman will love me as her partner one day in the future. Or, maybe I should call my wife and apologize and beg her to take me back."

"Well, if we've got those three options, let's hold off on number one," Kirk wisely suggested. "And, we know that you shouldn't beg your wife to take you back, because you'd just be doing it to stop the pain. You don't even *want* to be with her."

He was right. I didn't want to be with her. I wasn't attracted to her, and I had made a solid decision to leave her for a new life…even though it hadn't turned out like I had planned.

"But, she *does* deserve an apology. You should tell her that you're sorry and ask for her forgiveness. That would go a long way in soothing your soul."

It was like a light went on in my head.

"I hadn't even thought about apologizing to her. You think I should, huh?"

"Yeah, of course you should. You need to apologize for how much you've hurt her and your kids."

My tears were starting to dry, and I was sobering up to the fact that I needed to take responsibility for my actions.

"You are totally right. I'm going to call her right now to see if she can meet."

I immediately got off the phone, and I dialed her number. I was shocked that she picked up and was willing to meet at 12 noon…within 2 hours of my call.

I'm Sorry
It was Saturday, May 3rd, and Laura and the kids were planning to attend a birthday party for the child of a family friend. We arranged to meet at a nearby park, and we both pulled up at the same time. The sight of her gaunt face with a somber expression was unnerving. The pain of my public departure and her continual physical and emotional care for the kids was getting to her…the loss of sleep and weight was taking its toll.

As we sat down at the concrete picnic table, she faced me squarely while I looked down the bench off into the distance…unable to bear the sight of the pain wrought across her face.

"First of all…thank you for taking time to meet with me." I glanced over at her, and she just continued to stare at me with an intensity in her eyes that I never saw in all our years of marriage.

I fumbled through my words inserting "ums" every chance I could get. Not only could I hold the Guinness world record for dropping the f-bomb, but I could hold a similar record for the number of "ums" in a single conversation.

I knew that I needed to take responsibility for my actions and actually articulate the words "I am sorry"…but I found myself winding my way through a long introduction.

"I…um…want…um…you to…um…know…um…"

I wanted her to know that I didn't expect anything from her in return. I told her that she could turn around and walk right back to the van without saying anything. I wasn't asking her to take me back or forgive me on the spot or anything extraordinary. I just wanted her to listen.

She continued to stare at me like a lioness protecting her cubs. The turmoil and chaos of life was overwhelming, and tears began to flood down my face as I spoke.

"I know that my choices were completely inappropriate and selfish. I realize that I have caused huge amounts of pain for you and the kids. I take full responsibility for all my actions, and…"

Here's where the three words come in that are so easy to say…but require great humility and compassion to truly mean.

"I am sorry."

I said it. In fact, I tried to say in as many ways as I possibly could.

"I'm sorry for being unfaithful to you. I'm sorry for breaking my promise. I'm sorry for publicly humiliating you. I'm just so sorry. I hope that you'll be able to forgive me some day."

The relief of coming clean was tremendous. It wasn't a feeling of ecstasy or delight or joy…it was a feeling of sorrow for all that I'd inflicted upon her. It was the feeling of a million pound load coming off my shoulders.

I secretly hoped the conversation would end with that, but it didn't. She had questions, and she wanted answers.

"Are you still in love with her?"

"Um…well…um…I'd say that I care about her, but I'm not in love with her. A lot of things have changed over the past few weeks, and I have to move on."

She kept asking questions, and I tried to dodge the land mines as best as I could. I didn't want to cause her more pain while I was still processing the loss of Samantha…and yet, I wanted to be honest as well.

There came a point when it was obvious that we were done with the conversation. She didn't have any more questions, and we would have just stirred up more pain by discussing it continually. As I drove away, I exhaled a sigh of relief and gave Kirk a call to re-cap the conversation.

I didn't feel like killing myself that afternoon…or night…or the next day. He was right. I *did* need to apologize to her, and I didn't even know it. My soul was crying out to come clean with the one whom I had hurt the most, and now my soul was resting in the comfort of the grace that God extends…even if my wife was unable to in the moment.

On Sunday, I spent several hours with Waverly and Emerson…and with Kirk, my chaperone for the day. After a fun time together, we piled in Kirk's car for the 25 minute journey to drop them back off at home in Lakewood. I gave them the usual hugs and kisses goodbye, but this time it was different. I was starting to feel even more things change inside of me. It had only been 24 hours since I apologized to Laura, but something was causing major shifts within my head and heart.

As I got back into the car, I knew that I had to share all of this with Kirk. What erupted was a long monologue…

"I feel like I really need to re-frame my time in Newport Beach. I can't just mope around and feel sorry for myself. I'm not going to put on sack-

cloth and ashes as if my life was over because of what I've done wrong.

I think I'm supposed to think of this time as 'summer camp.' Not to downplay the seriousness of what I've done or the work that I need to do, but summer camp was always a time of exploration and learning as a kid. Sure, you were bummed to leave home, because you were sent away from family and friends. But, you got to meet new people and do things that you were never able to do back at home. You were able to be adventurous and try new things. That's what I need to do. I need to take advantage of my freedom to do whatever I want to do…not in a sinful way…but in a way that helps me find the real me.

And yet, there was always one thing true about summer camp…I hate to even say it…but you always went home. And…I think…well…I think I'm supposed to go home."

I didn't want to admit it, but I said it out loud. I had this inkling that it was in my future even if I didn't even want to go home in that moment. The monologue continued…

"If God really is who I've preached He is, then God is a God of redemption and reconciliation. His very best plan is to see broken relationships restored. Although He may let other people have the opportunity to be with another spouse, I don't think He's going to let me do that. I think He's going to pigeonhole me until I humble myself and do the work on my marriage that I should have been doing for the past 15 years. He's not going to let me have an intimate relationship with any person other than the woman that I originally covenanted to be with."

It came gushing out of me like a firehouse under years of pressure. As he always does, Kirk affirmed my positive intentions, and we processed what all that may look like.

"David, you've got to realize that you were so thirsty for connection that you were willing to drink anything in sight. You were even willing to drink mud. Yeah, it was satisfying to you…because there was moisture in it. You see, having a relationship with Samantha was great, because you were finally connecting with someone...but it wasn't genuine or long-lasting...not like it can be with your wife if you want it to be."

He was right. I was thirsty...parched in fact. All those years of over-working and overexerting myself in ministry had sucked me dry. Ministry didn't suck me dry. My search for significance and success did.

That night, I went back to my apartment, and I wrote Laura an email. I included all of what I had shared with Kirk, and I told her that I was setting the trajectory of my heart back toward her. She may never want me back, but I was willing to do my part to work on our marriage and be a great Dad.

Before hitting 'send,' I thought I should run it by Kirk. In his wisdom, he edited out the parts about me not being attracted to her anymore and still having feelings for Samantha.

I checked my email several times over the next few days, but she never responded. When I went to pick up the kids on Tuesday with my chaperone, I asked if she got the email.

She responded with, "Yep." She didn't even stop putting away the groceries long enough to look at me.

"I'm just taking it all in," she said.

I didn't have the guts to say anything else. I didn't want to cause any more problems, and I thought I'd just wait it out. But, she could have at least thanked me...geez.

As I continued to check my email for some sort of response from her, I kept getting those eHarmony matches. As my interest in "trying on" the dating life severely waned, I started hitting delete rather than even taking a look at the photos. Yet, one particular match caught my eye.

Before looking at her name, I noticed that she was a teacher at a Christian school in Costa Mesa, had two kids, and her face looked very familiar.

"Where do I know her from?" I thought.

The name read...Janice Latimore.

"Craaaaap! I got matched with Ron's ex-wife!"

I hit delete so fast on that email somehow thinking that I could make it all just go away. Then, I realized that she received an email with my profile.

"Does she even know that I'm not with Laura anymore? Will she think that I'm trying to hook up with some chick on eHarmony while I'm still married?"

Well, I guess I was still married...technically. I hadn't even shared with Kirk, Ron, or Dyno that I was on eHarmony, and now this happened. What a mess.

I called Ron to share the news, and he laughed harder than any human being I've ever heard.

"Dude, what are the chances of you getting matched up with my ex-wife? Out of the hundreds of thousands of people on that site, and you guys got connected." He burst out laughing even louder. "Well...you totally have my permission to date her if you want."

"No, thanks." I was laughing by this time, and I hoped that it would all just go away.

Unfortunately, it didn't.

A couple of days later, I got a text message from Kirk.
"Did you get connected with someone that we all know?"

I dialed his number immediately.

"Did *she* call you?" I asked.

"She who?"

"Janice Latimore!" I wondered why he was even asking.

"Um...no...but your *wife* did."

"Crap!"

"How did she find out?" I knew I was screwed.

"Janice called her and said that you guys got hooked up on eHarmony and that you had photos of your kids on your profile. She just wanted to give Laura a heads up about that."

"Oooh, man."

"Yeah, you may want to take those photos down," Kirk suggested.

"Well, I had already been planning on deleting my profile, but I just hadn't gotten around to it."

Let's just say that I went home that night and immediately deleted the profile and sent Laura an email apologizing for it all. I tried to explain the whole "trying-on-the-single-life" to her, but I'm not sure that even helped...probably just added salt to the wound.

Finding the New Me
Finding the new "me" started out with flip-flops, colored underwear, and a tanning booth. Those things were breakthroughs in freedom for me, but I wanted even more. I was finally coming to the place of being able to say, "I can do whatever I want to do."

No longer was I restricted by the responsibilities of being a pastor. Neither did I need to play into the opinions of others...especially since many people were so angry with me. And, I didn't even have the time constraints of being a husband and father each day since I was living on my own now.

Once I was liberated from all these encumbrances, I found that the re-
strictions I believed were around me were in fact figments of my own
imagination. I had put them in place or agreed for others to put them
there. When I felt stuck, I would do crazy things to get the freedom I
needed. I was starting to realize that I had to stay in a place where I'm
free all the time.

Freedom...utter and complete freedom is what I truly wanted. Once the
desire to kill myself faded, I found the new freedom exhilarating. I was
ready to find the new me.

I started wearing contact lenses...having worn glasses for over 10 years.
I bought a pair of sunglasses...rather than squinting at the sun. I shaved
off most all of my hair...and lost the curly locks. I bought clothes that
were slim...rather than the baggy ones that hung loose. I started talking
to people I didn't know...rather than feeling nervous and odd. I began to
go to the beach regularly...instead of avoiding it like I had since college.

When I saw people in public who I *did* know, they didn't even recognize
me. I told them I was in the "ex-pastor protection program" or that I was
on the "affair and divorce" diet.

I was growing more and more comfortable with my failures, but most
people who knew me in the past were not. That's one of the things that
Randy and I started working on...understanding my strengths and weaknesses...and accepting them no matter what others thought.

"David, the more you embrace the *total* you...the more you'll be comfortable being around anyone. When someone points out one of your
strengths, you can thank them with appreciation. When someone con-
fronts you on a weakness, you don't have to become defensive, because
you already have accepted that. It's old news!"

Frankly, I was more comfortable acknowledging my strengths than
weaknesses.

I am passionate and wacky.
I am a good leader and a creative communicator.
I am a visionary and a strategist.
I can see the creative, big picture and all the steps of how to get there.
I don't mind stepping up to lead…in fact, that's where I want to be.

Yet, I can also be a pain in the ass. Even Randy said so.
"You can be incredibly brilliant...and a big jerk."

Thanks Randy…appreciate that. Yet, it *is* true. I can definitely act that way. I can be very hard to work with, and I can micro-manage like there's no tomorrow. I like things done my way, and I probably won't agree with you unless you've got strong evidence to back up your perspective. If you're not doing it the right way, I'll tell you, and I probably won't be that tactful.

Those definitely tend to be my weaknesses, but I'm on a life-long journey to minimize them. I learned a long time ago that I need to embrace all of who I am…but I need to *build* on my strong points. The truth is I'll never be able to turn my weaknesses into strengths.

Ironically, the more I embraced my own strengths…the more I could celebrate the strengths of others without becoming threatened. And, the more I could embrace my own weaknesses…the less I criticized others for their shortcomings. Instead, I had compassion for them…knowing that I had weaknesses as well.

Part of discovering myself was getting a brain scan from the Amen Clinic started by Dr. Daniel Amen. I remembered that Kirk had gotten one a number of years back after his life melted down, and he strongly recommended it to me after I got out of the hospital. Essentially, they measure the activity level in your brain, and they look to see what parts are under or over-active based on a normative scale.

Kirk connected me with a foundation that often sponsored Christian leaders who were in a similar situation as mine. I submitted the paperwork, and they approved me for a full scholarship. In preparation, I read

Amen's best-selling book called "Change Your Brain, Change Your Life," and I was scared to death that they were going to discover I had axe-murderer tendencies.

Thankfully…they didn't.
Instead, they discovered two areas of my brain were working overtime.

Working with a therapist named Dr. Earl Henslin, I found out that my basal ganglia…controlling 'fight or flight'…was extremely overactive. In fact, I was hitting the upper end of their scale.

"So…when someone brings you negative information, you probably feel like running out of the room or pulling out a cannon and blowing them away?"

Yeah.

"You probably have a hard time shutting down your brain and resting."

Yep.

"And, bright lights and the sound of your kids probably drives you nuts…"

Uh-huh. How could this guy know that stuff?

He also saw that my cingulate…the 'gear-shifter' of your brain…was over-active as well.

"Well, that probably means that you can focus on something really well. In fact, you probably can't *stop* focusing on something…like work… and worry."

Um…yeah.

"You have the natural brain chemistry to be an incredible entrepreneur… and that has a tendency to kill relationships."

Ya think?

"I'm going to recommend that we start you on an anti-anxiety medication that should help slow down these parts of your brain. After a couple of weeks, we'll see if that's made a difference for you."

Great...I'm an official psycho. Not only have I been in a mental hospital, but I'm now going to be taking meds.

"I want you to know that you didn't choose your brain chemistry. You didn't choose for these parts of your brain to be over-active, but you do need to take responsibility for it. If not, you'll keep having the same relational challenges you've had for years."

To hear Dr. Henslin describe my brain was both unnerving and invigorating. I finally heard someone explain why I felt the way I did. Until that point in time, I thought everyone dealt with the same thoughts and feelings.

Doesn't everyone worry incessantly about the future? Doesn't everyone else have a never-ending buzz in their brain that makes them constantly think about accomplishing something? Doesn't every person want to punch the throat of anyone who stands in their way of that goal?

I guess not. I should probably fill that prescription.

STARTING OVER

Meds became my new friend rather quickly. Within a couple of weeks, I couldn't believe how I felt. My brain quit racing through a list of things that I could be doing instead of having a conversation with whomever I was talking with. I could think more clearly, and I didn't feel the need to be doing something just for the sake of activity. I could relax and be in the moment, and I started enjoying life for the first time in over 15 years.

I didn't even know that I could feel this way.
Alive. Present. Connecting.

As I was having dinner with a former Revolution Church leader, Chris Koble, for the first time since everything imploded, I could feel the difference of my new life. It was like someone slowed down my mind and allowed me to just look him in the eyes. I wasn't anxious about what he thought of me or what he was going to say. I was able to simply be with him in the moment.

After we assembled our Mongolian BBQ and it was cooked in front of us, we walked back to our table.

"David, I'm glad to be having dinner with you. I gotta tell you…I've missed you."

"That's good to hear in light of how much I've screwed things up. I'd like to share a bit of my story with you tonight. What do you think?"

It's the only way I knew how to convey all that had gone on in my life. A simple "I'm sorry" just didn't seem to suffice. It's not as though my story was offered as some sort of excuse, but it was my effort to share from the deepest part of my being…something that I hadn't done in the past.

As a pastor, it's easy (if not necessary) to stay in the role of a leader… which is excruciatingly difficult to intermingle with being a friend. If I'm trying to start and grow a church, I'm going to need to develop relationships with people in order to rally them to be part of the vision… which means that I'm going to enroll them in participating, serving, and investing financially. I found that many people thought we were just being friends and ended up feeling "used" in the process.

Unfortunately, I never figured out a way to be a leader of a church and everyone's friend. I'm not even sure it's possible. All I know is that I was sick and tired of connecting with people while I had a constant underlying motive…trying to move them forward in their involvement at the church.

While I was sitting there with Chris, I could feel something changing. I shared my story with him from the beginning to that very moment…just as I had with Sharon, the gal I poured my heart out to at the coffee shop. He listened intently, and he was compassionate toward my pain.

"Chris, I want you to know how sorry I am for making these selfish decisions. I wish I could take everything back and make it all go away, but I can't. The only thing I can do is make amends by living a new life now." He was incredibly gracious and forgiving.

For the first time in the four or so years that I knew Chris, I felt like I was *really* his friend. He probably had tried to be my friend in the past, but I was too busy being his leader. I didn't need to check in on his relationship with God. I didn't need to see how his participation in a small group or ministry team was going. All I needed to do was be present... to love and be loved.

I drove back to my apartment with a warm feeling that evening...a warmth of friendship.

Seeing Suresh Kumar Again

With summer around the corner, I knew that Suresh Kumar would be visiting southern California from India as he does each year. Normally, I would have him speak at Revolution Church since we were so invested in our partnership with Harvest India, and we'd take up a special offering for a specific humanitarian project that Suresh was leading. This summer was obviously going to be different.

Over the 10 years we had known each other, Suresh and I developed a wonderful connection, and I loved spending time with him. Yet, because of my relationship with Samantha, which started in India, I wondered if I'd ever see him again.

I wondered if he would ever want to see me.

I assumed that Kirk was in contact with him regularly, but I was too afraid to ask about the situation. Frankly, I didn't think I could handle much more rejection. Finally, I got up the courage to ask.

"Kirk, I know Suresh is going to be in town in the next couple of weeks. Do you think he'd be willing to sit down to meet with me?"

"Actually, he's already asked me to set that up."

"Really?" I was amazed.

"Yeah, he wants to spend time with you, and he's excited about what's going on in your life."

I was relieved to say the least. I didn't need an Indian contingent coming over to the US to remind me of my sin. People in my own backyard had done a good enough job of that.

The day finally arrived, and Suresh walked in to the coffee shop near my apartment. His warm embrace and bright smile were soothing to my soul. As I shared my story with him, I felt such deep shame over my choice to connect with Samantha in India. My selfish decisions not only impacted my family, but they had impacted his.

After getting word from Revolution, Suresh had to explain to his key leaders about my adultery. To know that I had disappointed the people of such an amazing organization that I had helped over the years was heartbreaking. To know that Revolution was now financially unable to support Harvest India because of the decline in giving as I left was devastating.

"Suresh, I am so sorry. I am so sorry that I have caused you and your staff pain. I am so sorry that my actions have caused a financial impact on Harvest India. I hope that you'll be able to forgive me someday."

"David, you are forgiven." With his thick Indian accent, Suresh poured out his heart to me. "In the family of God, there is grace and forgiveness. That is what Jesus modeled for us. Because we have been forgiven by Him, we are called to forgive others. You are forgiven *completely*."

His unbelievable grace and mercy was overwhelming, and it was hard to accept. His words were overflowing with love and a belief in me. It was like I was living in a dream.

"I believe that God is going to use all of these things in a powerful way. You will not be the same leader you were. You are going to impact even more. Mark my words. They will come true."

Suresh's words were an echo of what I had heard from Ron's mouth, and I was starting believe them…a little bit. I didn't believe that I was some tremendous person who God was fortunate enough to use. No… the exact opposite was true. I was feeling so humbled that I would be incredibly fortunate if God ever wanted to use me to do something positive on this Earth again.

"Suresh, would you be willing to speak with Laura while you're here? I think it would help her in some way."

"I already planned on it."

An Awkward Anniversary

Our 14th wedding anniversary was soon approaching, and I didn't want to just let it pass by. Although Laura and I weren't connecting more than when I picked up and dropped off the kids with the help of my chaperones, I wanted to make an effort to honor our relationship. I didn't know if we'd ever reconcile, but I needed her to know that I appreciated the good things we had experienced together over the years.

I didn't want to make a misstep in such a crucial time, so I turned to the one person who I knew could help…Kirk's wife. Having walked a similar road over seven years ago, I knew that she would have wisdom on what would be appropriate for such an occasion.

"Nothing too extravagant…no jewelry…just flowers…*not* red roses… but a nice bouquet would be great."

Okay, if I'm going to get her flowers, they need to be amazing, and I want to add something that's truly meaningful. Since they don't have a "I-cheated-on-my-wife-and-I'm-trying-to-reconcile" section, I tried to find the most appropriate anniversary card Hallmark carries. With the card chosen, I picked up the incredible bouquet of white flowers, and I headed toward our home.

I had been thinking for a few days about the "meaningful" part. Although flowers and a card are nice, I wanted to show her that I was serious about our relationship.

Within weeks after I left, she started asking for the key to the house back. She said that she didn't feel comfortable with me holding on to it. She didn't want me coming in whenever I pleased, and she'd feel safer with it in her possession. I hated hearing that she'd feel "safer" in some way. It made me feel like a monster that she was trying to protect herself from.

I knew what I needed to do.
I knew what I *wanted* to do.

After writing a short note about my appreciation for her, I got out of my car and walked to the front door. Since she was teaching at school during the day, I knew she wouldn't be at home. I slid the key into the lock and turned the knob. I walked in and carefully placed the large vase of flowers in the center of the dining room table.

I leaned the card against the vase, and I did one of the most romantic things I've ever done before.

I left the key to *her* house on the table.

End of the School Year
As the year was winding down, Laura and the kids were preparing for "Open House" at school. Laura was getting her class' work displayed all around the room, and Waverly and Emerson were completing special projects for each of them to display in their own classrooms.

In preparation for the night, Laura felt like it would be best if I simply met them at school, and I could walk around with the kids to their classes. Laura needed to be there early, so she dropped off the kids with some of our friends who would be joining us that evening.

To know that I wouldn't be the one who would drive my own kids to

Open House was so difficult. To see them walk up with another family in order to meet me was both humiliating and painful. I felt like I had failed as a dad, and now I was just being given the opportunity to tag along with chaperones once again.

When I walked out of the courthouse that day, I made a conscious decision to honor her request for a chaperone and prove to her and myself that I was a great dad...or at least becoming one.

Open House wasn't much different than any other time I connected with the kids. On most occasions, the chaperone brought the kids to me or I met them somewhere. To see my chaperones drive up with my kids in their car to meet me was not only awkward, but sad.

This was no one's fault other than my own.

I made the choice to leave my wife for another woman. I kept telling myself that I didn't leave my kids...just my wife. But, that's not true. When I chose to drive to San Diego with Samantha on that Friday in March, I was not only leaving Laura, but I was leaving Waverly and Emerson.

They would come home that night and ask where I was. Laura would be the one who would have to tell them the truth...not me. I was completely and utterly selfish to walk away from my commitment as a husband and my day-to-day role as a father by moving out of our family's home to move in with another woman.

I didn't think that life would take this turn.

I thought I'd be living comfortably with Samantha and making the new relationship with a total of six kids work out somehow. I didn't plan on Samantha leaving me. I didn't foresee losing my ability to function in the process. I didn't envision myself freaking out at Jamie or melting down in the car with Emerson. I didn't count on the possibility of ending up in the hospital with an intense desire to die.

Yet, that's exactly what happened.

After touring both Waverly and Emerson's classrooms, we ended up in
Laura's room as she wrapped up her conversations with several parents.
After offering to help clean up her room, I started to stack chairs on top
of desks in preparation for the nightly cleaning. With nothing else left to
do, I joined the kids near the play area in her classroom where they were
building Legos.

When I set the trajectory of my heart toward Laura, I was devoid of any
romantic feelings toward her. I cared about her as the mother of our children and a woman who I had been married to...but I didn't feel *in* love
with her. I trusted that what Kirk kept telling me was true.

"Make the choice to love her and the feelings will follow."

That night as I laid on the carpet and put Legos together with my kids,
I looked up at her organizing her classroom. As she chatted with our
friends, Laura reflected on the kids in her class, and a smile formed on
her face.

I felt something.

It was a goose-bumpy feeling inside of me that I hadn't felt in a long
time. It was a moment when I saw her in a new light...a light that allowed me to embrace both her strengths and weaknesses.

Laura is absolutely stunning...a gorgeous, healthy woman.
She is the most caring person I've ever met. She is faithful to the core.
She is a wonderful friend even when others aren't a friend to her.
She is an incredible teacher who loves kids more than any person I know.
She cares for Waverly and Emerson in ways that are truly sacrificial.
She is amazing!

On the other hand, she can also be rather messy. She follows the rules
too much, and she cares about the opinions of others when she doesn't
need to. And, she lets other people take advantage of her way too often.

The truth is that she has significant weaknesses.

That night, the light didn't just illuminate her strengths. It was as if I could see all of her at once...strengths *and* weaknesses...and feel a genuine love for her. I felt a love for her just the way she was, not the way she could be.

Trying to Make a Living

If Laura was ever going to take me back, I knew I had to start making a living to support our family once again. I still didn't want to get a regular 9 to 5 job that would chain me to a desk and provide $35,000 for a guy with 10 years of ministry experience. I just had to find a way to make money and stop living on my credit card.

Ron got me involved in enrolling telephone technicians in technical classes at Chapman University, but I was a complete failure. It just didn't work out how we all planned, and I ended up wasting hours and hours of time with no compensation. In some ways, I think the "work" was a Divine gift to keep me busy when I could have been sitting around plotting ways to kill myself.

John Weeks and I were scheming about launching a Facebook-style website for tweens, but we were never able to raise more than $100,000 to get started. It just didn't feel like things were coming together, so the concept dwindled in our minds.

Because of all the marketing experiences that I had gained through starting a church, I had become rather proficient in thinking strategically about communications and about directing the creative process. Kirk suggested that I design and build a couple of websites for non-profits that he was involved in, and he would pay me. I jumped on that offer immediately.

A few more websites later, and I started thinking that this could actually be a way to earn some income. I wasn't sold on it as a career path, but I thought it could help in the meantime while I was figuring out what I really wanted to do. Since Kirk had so many contacts in Orange County and I had the ability to direct the creative process, we decided to team up to start our own boutique marketing studio called 8TRACKstudios. After getting our business license and landing a couple of clients, we hired a part-time project manager and a part-time graphic designer and developed a plan. We launched a website and sent out a promotional brochure to 500 or so contacts. We were in business!

At the same time, a small non-profit Kirk was running was in need of a part-time team member that could manage projects, events, and marketing. I jumped on the opportunity to work with Kirk in this capacity, and the income was a true godsend for my bank account.

I spent way more time meeting with contacts and potential clients than actually ever doing much work for 8TRACKstudios, but it did occupy my mind and my time. Unfortunately, it didn't pay the bills. Whatever money came in went to our employees or to personal projects we were working on, and that wasn't going to work very long for me...or especially for Laura.

Thank God For Kids Getting Sick

I had grown accustomed to chaperones tagging along with me and the kids, and I actually grew to enjoy it. I had a great time including whoever it was into our family time, and I encouraged them to bring their kids along as well.

Unfortunately, that didn't always work out.

On one particular Tuesday evening, I got a call from one of my chaperones informing me that her daughter was sick, and she wasn't going to be able to accompany us for the night.

"Do you want me to call someone else to see if they can join you?" she asked.

"No, I have a better idea. Why don't you call Laura and tell her that your daughter is sick...then suggest that she could be my chaperone for the evening instead."

"I don't know if I should do that. Will she go for it?"

"I don't know, but it's worth a try." I was a taking a chance here. This could go really good...or really bad. It turned out that Laura was up for it, and she met me at the mall to have dinner with the kids.

As we sat down at the table, I decided to take a leadership role...which I would have never had taken in the past. I would have opted to let her help the kids figure out what they wanted to order, and she would have completely taken care of their needs.

This time, I jumped in...and she let me.
She remained quiet and reserved.
She seemed to be watching my every move.

As the kids and I normally did, we took time to share our "highs and lows" from the day...something that was great and something not-so-great.

Waverly couldn't wait to share.
"My high is that we're having dinner together as a family tonight."

"Me, too!" Emerson agreed.

Laura and I looked at each other, and it seemed to be the opening I was looking for. After dinner, we walked around the mall, and Laura gave me some space to enjoy being with the kids. At the end of the night, it was hard to say good-bye...knowing that they'd head back home and I'd head to my empty apartment.

I hugged the kids, and my family drove away.

Long Calls Late Into the Night
Within days, Laura called to talk. She didn't really call to have a conversation, but it was more a need on her part to get some things off of her chest.

"I just need to say a few things, and I don't need you to respond. Just listen."

She went on to pour out her heart about how hurt she was about my decision to be with Samantha, her best friend. She felt completely betrayed by both of us, and she was in so much pain. She didn't know if she could ever trust me again, and she was feeling so angry about the entire situation.

I just listened.
I didn't say a word.
I just made enough affirmative sounds to ensure that she knew I was listening.

I took it all in. I wanted to know the depth to which I had wounded her. I felt great sorrow for what I had done, and I was willing to do whatever was needed in order to earn her trust back.

She asked me a few questions, and I tried to answer them as sensitively and honestly as possible. After I got off the phone, I felt a cleansing inside. It was like wounds from the past were being cleaned. It hurt, but I knew it was going to lead to health no matter what the outcome of our marriage was going to be.

We continued to talk from time to time, and some calls went late into the night. Although we were processing the past, it was like we were starting over in some ways. I did my best to share vulnerably about all that I was learning, and I was amazed by Laura's willingness to dig deep into her own life. In no way was Laura to blame for my choice to have an affair, but she was willing to take responsibility for her part in our marriage.

"I need to get healthy for *me* whether we choose to be together or not."

She kept saying this from the beginning of our re-connection. She was focused and passionate about learning all that she could about her own life. She wasn't the meek and mild Laura I had been used to over the past 15 years. She was feisty and able to stand up for herself…and I loved it!

Eventually, I got up enough guts to ask her out on a date.

"Um...if you ever want to...um...go out to dinner, I'd love the opportunity to take you. No pressure...um...but know that the offer stands."

Through conversations with Kirk and Randy, I made up my mind to let
her set the pace for our relationship. I have the tendency to take things
so fast in life that I can run people over. I wanted her to be in the driver's
seat when it came to taking next steps. Eventually, she *did* take me up
on the offer.

It was a Friday night, and she arranged for a sitter. I wanted to make the
night special for her, and I wanted to share my love for her in a creative
way.

A vintage book of love poems.
White paint and a paintbrush.
An Exacto knife and Sharpee.
Red ribbon.
And, a new iPod.

After loading the iPod with a playlist of songs just for her, I cut out a
spot in the middle of the book to place the iPod and earbuds. Carefully
cutting a square through a hundred or more pages, the hiding spot was
complete. After painting the surface of the first 10 pages, I wrote the
name of each song on a page with the key line from the lyrics below the
cutout. Once everything was dry, I placed the iPod in the book, and I tied
the red ribbon around it. My gift was ready.

After getting showered, I sprayed on some cologne...something Laura
loves me to wear. I got dressed and headed her way for the big night. I
felt the same way back in 1993 as I prepared for our first date...nervous
and excited. I couldn't wait to be alone with her, but I also dreaded the
potential questions that could arise.

I picked her up, and we drove to 2nd Street in Belmont Shore, a trendy
area near the water. After parking the car, I pulled out the book from

underneath my seat.

"Laura, I wanted to give you a special gift tonight…"

I handed her the old, musty book of poetry, and she tried to muster up a smile.

"You may want to untie the ribbon."

She carefully pulled on the bow and opened the book to see the song listed on the first page. "I loaded a few songs just for you."

The look on her face was worth all the time cutting out those stinkin' pages and slicing open my thumb in the process. We listened to a couple of the songs as we shared earbuds, and then she gave me a hug…a hug that I'll never forget.

This was the first physical touch we experienced since the week I left home. There's something powerful about touching another human being. The connection that comes from physical touch is unlike any other. It can draw you closer…or tear you apart.

We enjoyed a long, intimate conversation over dinner that evening. Her questions and my answers produced tears in the eyes of both of us. I didn't have anything to hide. I made the decision to share everything she wanted to know. Sometimes the answers weren't what she wanted to hear, but they were the truth.

As we walked down the street that night to browse in the shops, she reached out and took me by the hand. I couldn't believe it. I was walking down the street with the woman who I publicly betrayed four months prior, and she was willing to hold my hand. Not only was she willing, but she initiated the connection.

As her fingers slipped between mine, I was reminded of Randy's definition of love that he shared with us during our pre-marital counseling.

"Love isn't about fireworks and ecstasy. Love is the gnarled hands of an elderly man and woman as they hold one another until the very end."

Although our young hands were far from "gnarled," his picture of love as a commitment to be with one another through it all was glimmering in my mind's eye.

In the months prior, I had felt the euphoria of holding someone else's hand, but that didn't last forever. What does last is the richness of a deep commitment to love my wife through all that life brings our way. What does last is an intimacy that can only be nurtured by doing the hard work of sharing myself with her.

Counseling Leads to Connection

Soon after we began re-connecting via the phone and in person, I wanted to make myself available to begin marriage counseling when she was ready. Once again, I didn't want to push anything, but I wanted to ensure that she knew I was willing to work hard on the relationship.

Although we could have found a new therapist, Laura was comfortable going to see Randy despite the fact that I had been seeing him on an individual basis for the past few months. She knew he wouldn't be "taking my side" at any point in time, and we were both quite comfortable with him since we've known him for over 18 years.

Week after week, we met at Randy's office to work on our relationship. He checked in on Laura's healing process, and he ensured that I was staying on track as I learned how to develop intimate relationships with Laura, the kids, and several friends. She was learning to be strong and stand up to me as I was figuring out how to throttle back and find my identity in other things besides work, accomplishments, and success.

The counseling was healing the wounds of the past and helping us see the potential of a new future together.

When we began, Laura still wasn't sure that she wanted to be with me. She needed to see more evidence of my personal growth and commitment to our family. She wanted to see me continue to take positive steps in my own health and transformation. Thankfully, she saw that I was serious about making changes in my life. And over time, we started to connect more and more.

One night as we were ready to say good-bye at the end of an evening together, she leaned over to give me a hug.

"I want you to know that you don't need to have a chaperone with the kids anymore. The three months isn't up yet, but I don't want you to have to worry about it. You've been doing an amazing job with the kids, and I see that."

Tears began to well up in my eyes and stream down my face. I felt as if I crossed a finish line of a race that I never set out to run. I chose to honor her request from the beginning, and I never spoke negatively about the situation. My character was formed through the experience, and she was affirming my choices.

The relief in that moment was overwhelming. To be able to pick up my own kids to take them to dinner was incredible. What I was bothered by in the past seemed completely insignificant in the present.

When they talked too much, I was happy to hear their voices. When they fought, I saw it as a teaching moment. When they asked me for everything, I was excited to even be asked. I was just happy to be with them.

As I dropped them off after each visit, Laura began inviting me in to help with their bedtime routine. The opportunity to help them get bathed and ready for bed was a complete and total privilege. What used to feel like an interruption and a nuisance was now a joy!

After we prayed with both of them separately in their rooms, there was an initial awkwardness. On the first occasion, I rushed out of the house rather abruptly so that I wouldn't have deal with the pain of her encouraging me to leave.

On the next occasion, she asked me to stay. We sat on the couch and talked and talked for several hours. We were connecting at such a deep level, and it was becoming apparent what she did and did not want.

She didn't want a workaholic husband anymore.
She wanted a nurturing man who would lead our family as a servant.
She didn't want a husband more committed to ministry than to her.
She wanted a faithful man who would sacrifice for the sake of family.
She didn't want a husband who sat around surfing the Internet.
She wanted a participating man who would help shoulder the load of a home and kids.

I ended up driving 30 minutes from Newport Beach to Lakewood more nights than not during the week. Although it wasn't *my* night to hang with the kids, Laura was inviting me up to participate in their lives more and more often.

After the kids would go to bed, we'd just sit and talk. With all this intimate heart connection, I knew that something more was going to happen sooner or later…but I wanted her to initiate.

On that night when she finally leaned over and gave me a kiss, it was like electricity shot through my entire body.

There wasn't much of the typical romantic stuff present.
No music or candles or rose petals or wine.
Just a lot of forgiveness and grace and mercy.

Within the next week, she took me by the hand and led me into what used to be *our* bedroom. My nightstand and lamp were gone, and she had taken over the entire closet. There was a new dresser and nightstand on her side of the bed, and what used to be my side was pushed almost all the way to the wall.

It was now *her* bedroom…and she was inviting me in.

As she slowly unbuttoned my shirt and removed my clothes, I was reminded of the intimacy of our first night together after our wedding. The awkwardness, the love, the passion.

This wasn't a "tear-her-clothes-off" kind of moment. This was an honor to be back in the arms of the woman who I had betrayed at the deepest level.

As I looked upon her naked body...excessively thinned by the worry and strife of it all...I was humbled by her grace. She wrapped her arms around me and pulled my nakedness close to her. The warmth of her chest against my cheek as I listened to her heartbeat was tender. As we made love that night, tears rolled down the sides of her cheeks in memory of all the pain. I wiped them away with my hands one by one...tending to the wounds of the one I had wounded.

Although I wanted to stay, I knew that it wasn't the right time. I stood up out of bed and got dressed once again. After hugging and kissing her goodnight, I drove all the way back to Newport Beach.

This scene replayed several times in the coming days, and I was growing weary of leaving what I wanted to be *our* home once again.

Will I Stay or Will I Go?
Soon enough, it became evident that we would need to have a discussion about me possibly moving back into our family's home. Since I was already there several nights a week, it was apparent to both of us that this was a topic of conversation for our counseling sessions.

With summer break around the corner for both Laura and the kids, Laura was definitely looking forward to the time off to continue processing our relationship. Me moving back in was a scary proposition for sure. This was not something I was going to rush, and I needed to let it simply unfold.

She had thrown out a timeline of six months or even until I was able to pay off the credit card. This topic came up in counseling quite quickly.

"I just can't see him returning home with over $30,000 on a credit card. I didn't go through all this to be saddled with that kind of debt."

This was a huge hot button for her.

Laura's family went through enormous financial turmoil when she was in high school including the time she had to move out of her house over a weekend because of a default on the mortgage.

We were always very careful with our finances...never having any debt except for our mortgage and one car loan. Credit card debt was a big "no-no" in our household, and I had obviously blown that.

A trip to San Diego, dinners, and lots of entertainment with Samantha.
Deposits and monthly rent for both the apartments.
Furniture and household items.
Clothes, car repairs, tanning booth visits, the removal of my braces.
And of course...Samantha's ring.

It was all on the card. It's amazing how fast $33,000 can rack up.

Laura talked long and hard in counseling about that one...and I tried to do more listening than anything else. In my head, I was thinking, "I'll never move back home if I have to pay off that card with the amount of money I'm making right now. I am screwed!" But, I kept my mouth shut, and I let Randy do the negotiating.

"Laura, maybe instead of making a decision about David moving home for good, why don't you just invite him to spend the night one time? This could feel like a trial run to see what it's like."

I liked the sound of that.

"David, would you be open to something like that?" Randy asked.

"What you don't know is that I've had a bag packed in the trunk of my car for two weeks. I've just been waiting for her to ask."

The room was silent.

"Wow…what do you feel when you hear David share that?"

"It tells me that he hasn't been pushing me…but he's been ready," Laura quietly said.

This was one of those moments in counseling when I wanted to stand up and yell, "Yeah baby! Look at my progress….Yeah!!!" But, I didn't. I sat there calmly taking it all in.

She was right. I had been ready. My bag had been packed for quite awhile. I was dying to spend the night back in our bed sleeping next to her. I was so looking forward to waking up in the morning and having breakfast with the kids. But, I didn't want to push. I was waiting for her.

A few nights after that counseling appointment, she asked…and it was amazing. The absolute privilege of sleeping with Laura and waking up with the entire family was unbelievable. I slept back at my own apartment the next night, but I hoped and prayed that it wouldn't be long before I could sleep in our bed once again.

A Change of Plans

Everything was right on track…or so I thought. I could see it by the look in her eyes. She needed to tell me something, and it probably wasn't going to be good. After being together for 15 years, I knew that look all too well.

"Babe, I need you to know there's been a slight change of plans…I'm pregnant."

I hadn't even moved home yet.

"How did this happen?" I begged for an answer that made sense.

"Well, I thought we were being careful, but I guess we weren't *that* careful."

Because of the circumstances, we weren't exactly excited to tell anyone. Our new relationship wasn't getting the grandest reception from people in our lives. Most people were protective of Laura...assuming that I had manipulated her into taking me back. They were trying to protect her from the "evil one." I had been demonized by so many people, which is rather common reaction in the church when a pastor blows it.

Some people who were genuinely interested in our well being kept asking us for an update. We ended up sending out a couple of emails to let people in on our progress, and we were met with a few "please removes" as well. Let's just say that people weren't exactly supportive when Laura quit being the patient they liked to protect and take care of...and actually became strong enough to take care of herself.

We began to process the new addition with our therapist, but we didn't tell hardly anyone else...not even our kids.

As our minds were just getting used to the idea of being parents for the third time, the plan changed once again.

Laura miscarried.

Although we would have warmly welcomed a third child into our lives, neither one of us felt like a new addition would be the best thing as we were reconciling our marriage. We were experiencing a mixture of relief and grief all at the same time. Having gone through two previous miscarriages in between the births of Waverly and Emerson, we knew what to expect...but it was still a difficult and painful process.

Camping and Construction

By the time July rolled around, Laura and the kids were planning their yearly camping trip with families from Revolution. I say *their* camping trip, because I had never gone. I'm not a big fan of camping, and I always found a reason to work in years past.

This year was different.

With my newfound freedom in life and openness to adventure, I was ready for anything that came my way...including the great outdoors. Unfortunately, I knew that I probably wouldn't be welcome. And, I was right.

Laura checked with a couple of the families who were leading the trip, and they all agreed that it would just be too awkward. Because I had not been given the opportunity to apologize to the leadership of Revolution, most people were stuck in that funky place of demonizing me. They didn't know that I was truly remorseful, and many questioned my motives no matter what I did.

The positive thing was that it gave me an opportunity to surprise my family when they returned.

Having developed a great deal of trust for me over the last two months, Laura gave me a new key to the house and permission to "do a few things" as I suggested. Within one week, I rallied a contractor to paint half of the house's interior including two bedrooms, the hallway, and the main bathroom. I installed ceiling fans in all three bedrooms and curtains on three windows in the living room. I framed the kids' artwork and a recent family photo and hung them on the wall. And, I had a landscaper put in a load of flowers in the front and back yards.

When my family arrived back home a week later, their eyes couldn't believe what was in front of them. It looked like a completely different home.

The joy of serving my family in this way was completely rewarding, and there was no sense of me *earning* my way back into good standing. I truly wanted to love them in a tangible way and have them experience the joy of a fresh environment in our home.

I say *our* home. Although my name was still on the loan, it was really *theirs*. In fact, after a week of intense work to transform the space, I had to drive back to my empty apartment on the night they arrived.

The loneliness of that ride home was like no other. I had invested so much time, energy, and money into the project, but I knew that it wasn't time for me to move back in yet. I had not been invited.

As we sat down for our next counseling session, Randy asked about the previous week. Laura went on and on about all my hard work and the excitement of the kids returning to a new space. It was priceless to hear her recognition and enthusiasm for all my hard work.

"Well, Laura, how are you feeling about Dave's transition back to the house?"

"I'm starting to feel better about it. I hate the fact that he has all that debt, but I don't want him to be away from our family any longer."

Randy leaned forward a bit and began to enter negotiation mode. I leaned backward and tried not to mess anything up...which I'm gifted at doing.

"What if we put some sort of timetable on Dave moving back in so that it can be something we work toward? Is there a date that would feel comfortable for you, Laura?"

"The kids and I did plan to go to Palm Springs for the week in early August...hmmm...maybe he could come out to be with us for a few days and then move back in the next week."

Although that was still a couple of weeks away, I was overjoyed. What could have been months of trying to pay down that debt turned into a great deal of grace on her part. In fact, there was no guarantee she would ever take me back.

Kirk, Ron, and Dyno kept reminding me of the type of woman I had married...an absolute class-act angel. What woman would be willing to reconcile with their husband after being publicly humiliated in such a horrible way? What woman would take the initiative to work on her own issues and health from the very beginning? What woman would be willing to allow so many friendships to die as she forgave and welcomed her husband back home?

Laura is an incredible woman, and I was choosing to deeply love her.

After a wonderful family vacation in Palm Springs, I started moving my stuff back in. A great deal of it had been recently purchased, but we just didn't need it. It ended up on the back driveway under a giant tarp in preparation for a huge yard sale.

Once again, I had to pay to break a lease…this time in Newport Beach. The financial cost was well worth it in order to move back in with the family I so dearly loved and missed.

Spending my first official night back at home was amazing…not because of some grand party or sex with my wife or breakfast in bed. It was simply amazing to feel the peace within my soul to be where I was supposed to be all along…back at home.

I had taken all the warmth and connectivity my home had to offer for granted. In fact, I'm not sure I ever allowed myself to experience it in the first place. The joy of waking up next to my wife and walking out into the living room to see my kids watching TV was comforting..

We were a family once again.

Confessing and Making Amends
As I moved back in, I knew that I needed to start confessing and making amends to some key people who were part of my life…first of which would be my kids. A quick "I'm sorry" at the dinner table didn't exactly feel appropriate. Laura and I both knew that it had to be the special moment.

One night as we were putting the kids to bed, it just felt right.

Laura and I sat down on Emerson's bed, and I apologized for how my decisions had hurt him and our family. At six years old, he didn't really comprehend or respond too much. He was just happy to have his wrestling partner back at home. On the other hand, I knew that Waverly was fully aware of the pain associated with my decisions.

"Waverly, I wanted to take a moment to chat with you." Laura was kneeling on the floor next to me as I sat on our 10 year-old's bed.

"As you know, Daddy made some really bad decisions over the past year." I was trying to find an appropriate way to start the conversation.

"Like being with Samantha?" she asked in an innocent voice.

"Yeah, like being with Samantha." My lips were quivering and tears welled up in my eyes. "I was completely wrong to leave Mommy to be with Samantha, and I know that I caused a lot of pain in our family."

She closed her eyes and grimaced.

"I want you to know how sorry I am. I hope that you'll be able to forgive me some day."

As she opened her eyes, she sat up in bed and reached out for me. I held her tightly in my arms as she cried on my shoulder. Tears were streaming down my face, and I couldn't bear to look over at Laura.

Knowing how much pain she had gone through, I was savoring the sweetness of the moment. I'm not sure if she forgave me at that point, but I knew we were connecting in ways that we never had in the past.

I only hoped that all my other conversations would go this well.

Since I had not been in contact with him at all, I also felt the need to re-connect with Rob Mason, my former boss. I sent Rob an email to request a meeting, and he quickly responded. Within a couple of days, I found myself sitting on the patio of a Starbucks telling my story once again. He was patient to listen and more gracious than I could have ever imagined. Being known as a hard-nosed leader who threatens to cut your balls off if you have an affair, Rob was showing an intense amount of restraint.

"You're forgiven. It's over, and let's put this behind us."

"Well, Rob, I'd really like to apologize to the Revolution staff or leadership community when you think it's the right time. I want to leave that up to you."

"They are definitely *not* ready. If you got up to say anything now, they'd eat you alive," he warned.

"Okay, okay...well, when you think they're ready."

Rob and I continued to connect from time to time, and everything went on as if nothing had ever happened. I asked him on a couple of more occasions about the timeliness of a confession and apology, but he still didn't think the church was ready.

He did end up encouraging me to sit down one on one with Michael, the Downey campus pastor who had shouldered a great deal of the weight since my departure. Our time together was as anticipated. I shared my story, and he got a chance to give me the tongue-lashing that he had been dying to unleash. Even though I was disappointed, I didn't really expect him to be able to handle the situation much differently.

Laura and I also pinpointed four couples who we wanted to begin to hang out with, and I initiated contact with them all. In fact, I met with each couple individually to share my story and apologize, and I was warmly welcomed on each occasion. With little or no friends left to hang out with, Laura and I looked forward to re-connecting with these four couples...two of which we were close to in the past and two of which were newer friendships...all from Revolution.

In the meantime, my dad contacted me about the possibility of meeting halfway between Lakewood and Sacramento to spend the night and talk through our relationship. Since that day at Black Angus when he told me I was a prodigal son, we hadn't interacted much...just a long letter from him and a response back from me.

There wasn't much reason to interact. He obviously didn't like my initial decision nor my desire to have the freedom to even make it. Although I continued to connect with my mom over the phone from time to time, I never spoke with my dad…but I knew that needed to change.

I was hesitant to spend the night in the same room with him. What if things weren't going well? Did I really want to try to go to sleep with a room full of tension? On the other hand, what kind of message would that send to my dad?

"Hey Dad, I'm totally up for talking through our relationship, but I want my own room."

Nope. I couldn't envision myself saying that, so I prayed that things wouldn't explode that night.

As we sat down for dinner at a cheap Mexican restaurant within walking distance of the hotel, it was obvious that we still didn't agree. I made it clear that I was not interested in having him prevent me from making a decision that he thought was reckless. I was sick and tired of tiptoeing around trying not to upset him, and I wanted the freedom to be "me." At the same time, he challenged me to let him keep his own opinions and not try to change him either.

I'm not sure we ever came to any conclusions that night other than we agreed to disagree from that point forward.

I did know this though. Although I loved my dad so much, I also wanted to have my own identity. I don't think I ever felt that freedom during my upbringing, but now I wanted it. I'm not sure he was trying to force me to be someone in particular so much as I was just feeling the natural pressure to please my dad.

There was no tension in the room as we both fell asleep that night. The next morning, we checked out, hugged one another, and said our good-byes. I knew that things would be different from that point forward.

I could be "me" even if he didn't approve.

From Mourning to Dancing

Since our reconnection, Laura and I began talking about hosting an event where we could renew our wedding vows. We didn't want to be one of those cheesy, pseudo-weddings where middle age people are just thanking God that they made it that far without killing each other.

We wanted to tell our story...the *entire* story.

With Randy's input, we crafted a dialogue between Laura and I that shared the intimate process of us meeting, getting married, growing apart, my implosion, and our reconnection. On the night of this event, 50 or so friends and family members joined us in the small sanctuary of a Long Beach church. With Laura standing on the left and me on the right, we told our story from beginning to end...confessing our weaknesses and sharing the Divine Grace interwoven through our reconciliation.

Kirk helped everyone process the brokenness of the moment, and Randy guided our friends and family through a time of celebration.

As we stood before our family and friends, Laura and I re-committed our lives to one another...not with great fanfare or fancy flowers...but against the backdrop of forgiveness.

Unfortunately, many of our relationships (including the four couples we specifically sought out) were unable to withstand the stress of the entire situation. The weeks afterward were telling of their ability to extend forgiveness toward me. Most of them simply couldn't handle the awkwardness of being in my presence...knowing what I had done so publicly.

Although Laura was welcoming me back into her life, most all of them couldn't...or wouldn't.

As the weeks passed and Laura and I developed a "new normal" for our lives, her list of friends continued to steadily wane. While I lost most of my relationships back in March from the moment I left my wife, Laura lost most of hers gradually as she welcomed me home.

Most people just couldn't handle it.

A New Normal

This new normal was a matter of choice. It wasn't as if we fell into a new pattern of life. We realized that there were certain things we had been doing…or I had been doing…that just weren't helpful to our relationship or our family.

It wasn't so much a matter of *stopping* certain activities.
It was more like *starting* new rhythms of life.

Instead of working on weekends at the church, I was now home to be with my family. I was committed to preserving this time as sacred. We wouldn't just sit around and watch TV and play video games. Our new normal would include "Trotter Family Adventures" where we went to new places to do new things…together.

Rather than working at night and eventually falling into bed with the TV on, we removed the relationship killer. Instead, we enjoyed our time with one another and fell asleep in each other's arms…without Letterman present in the bedroom.

In our old life, Laura would work full-time and take care of our home. Instead, I started doing all the grocery shopping, cleaning up after we made dinner together, and helping more with the kids.

Instead of going months without a night out as a couple, Laura and I committed to a weekly date night and a once a month counseling session. With a standing babysitter in place, this new normal was something that we looked forward to right away.

More than anything, our new normal started to feel like a partnership. Ironically, that's what I left Laura for in the first place.

I wanted a partner to raise kids, experience adventure, make a positive impact in the world, and enjoy living life with. Ironically, I had that partner right under my own roof. I was just too lazy to do the hard work to become a partner myself.

I was more willing to go through the pain of a divorce than make the needed changes in my own life to get the results I truly wanted.

A serendipitous reminder of my selfish, insane decisions reared its ugly head one day. As I sat in my home office working on a project, Laura walked up from behind and tossed a magazine on my desk.

"Take a look at *this!*"
I read the title..."Divorce Magazine."

A large photo of a woman hugging her daughter at the beach took up the entire front cover. It was Laura and Waverly.

The editors of this free, quarterly magazine chose a photo of my wife and daughter (taken by Shelley Pelosi right after I left) from the hundreds of thousands of images on iStockphoto. They had no clue what we had gone through, and yet this is the photo they chose. Thousands of magazines were distributed in stands in front of grocery stores throughout southern California.

Laura was getting calls and emails for months from people.

"Did you know that you and Waverly are on the front cover of a divorce magazine?"

"Yes, please go get them all and throw them in the trash," Laura responded...time after time.

This magazine cover was a Divine message.

"David, is this what you wanted? Did you *really* want to divorce your wife? Did you *really* want to leave your entire family?"

As I sat there and looked at the magazine cover, I got the message. It was like a punch in the gut. No, this is *not* what I wanted. I wanted an intimate relationship with my wife, and I'm going to do everything I can to develop that partnership.

I was choosing a new normal for my life.

Experiencing Lots of "Firsts"

Every new experience or event that came our way felt like a family "first." The scenery was more vibrant and the emotions more real. We were present with one another in a new way.

Waverly and Emerson were keenly aware of the transformation. They started to comment about their "new Daddy" and how different he was. We compared our old way of life with our new one on a regular basis.

Without the activity of leading a church and all the stress that goes along with it, I was now physically and emotionally present for all the holidays and special events. From Halloween to Christmas to the kids' school programs to a family vacation in Florida…I was finally present in a way that I wasn't before.

We also invited a few people to join us in starting a community of faith that would seek to follow the teachings of Jesus together. We were hesitant to call it a church and more comfortable calling it a community. We started gathering on Sunday mornings at our home to meditate and study together. The warmth of this group of fellow travelers was a well-needed addition to our lives.

With so many "firsts" going well, we even discussed the possibility of finally starting the children's home in India…and visiting it as a family for Christmas. This was quite an adventurous idea for a family with two kids addicted to cheese pizza and yogurt. We weren't sure how they'd deal with two weeks of curry and rice…and no access to a TV or the Wii. Yet, we all agreed that we really wanted to go.

The question was, "Is this the right time?"

In the midst of our discussion, we found out that the school district planned to let Laura go from her teaching job due to California budget cuts.

What were we going to do?
Would she be able to get a new job in another school district?
Or, would I have to ramp up my income somehow?

My income definitely wasn't enough to cover all the bills, and I was going to have to make some serious shifts with 8TRACKstudios in order to make that happen. After asking Kirk if I could continue on with the business as my sole focus instead of as a partnership, he agreed, and I started to generate more income immediately...but it wasn't going to be enough.

At the same time, Laura and I still wanted to start the children's home in India though. We knew in our hearts that it was the right thing to do. We knew that we could make some sacrifices if we needed to in order to get those kids into a safe environment.

We gave Suresh the go ahead to start the project by taking the children into the home, and we both had a peace about it all. We had a deep trust that God was going to provide somehow...some way.

With a week left before the school year was to begin, Laura was called in for an interview, and we were praying hard that she would get hired.

If she landed a job...I could finally get back on her insurance and stop paying the $400 a month for COBRA insurance like I had for the past 18 months. We wouldn't have to sell our house and move into a one-bedroom apartment. We wouldn't have to pick up bread from the food pantry down the street. And, we wouldn't have to get rid of the family mini-van.

All the while I had my eye on a black Mercedes to replace my old white Ford Focus. Although the Focus and I had been through a lot together... and I did enjoy the missing side-view mirror and broken headlight, there was something about that vision of me driving down Pacific Coast Highway that I just couldn't shake. I wanted Laura to be that blonde in the passenger seat of a new black Mercedes.

Laura was well aware of the vision I had in the hospital, and she was fully supportive as well. Unfortunately, our finances weren't "supportive" enough to afford a brand new Mercedes. We figured we could spend $400 a month on a payment if I could go back on her health insurance.

One small detail…Laura had to get a job first.

Almost 30 teachers in the district who had been laid off due to California budget cuts were called back for interviews. After Laura had a great first interview, she got a follow-up call from one of the principals.

Laura landed a job!

We couldn't believe that she was one of only three teachers who were hired back. Although she wouldn't be at the same school where our kids attended, she was able to continue teaching kindergarten, and we celebrated the Divine gift.

The day after she signed her contract I headed down to the Mercedes dealership. I had been researching the best car we could afford…a three-year-old Mercedes Benz C230. I pointed right to the car, and the salesman quickly showed up with the key.

I generally avoided luxury cars. I never wanted to ride in a friends' Mercedes or BMW or Infiniti or Lexus, because I knew that I'd want one. Now, I had the chance. Sure…it wasn't new…but it was nice…*very* nice.

The body was in perfect condition, and the black interior was in impeccable shape…simply gorgeous. As I sat down in the seat, it enveloped me with leather that was perfectly shaped to my body. All the new-fangled electrical stuff was overwhelming…steering wheel, sunroof, seats, windows, and even the rear headrests.

As I pulled out into traffic, I couldn't believe what I was feeling. The zippiness of my Focus didn't compare with the stability and power of the car in my vision. There was a reason why I never wanted to drive one of these cars, and I was experiencing it.

I was in love...and I called Laura to let her know.

"Babe, I found it."

"Found what?" she asked.

"I'm sitting in the black Mercedes that I want."

"Really?" She was surprised. "I just got a job, and you're already down there?" She wasn't really *that* surprised. She knew that I was a man of action.

"Of course I am. You know me. There's nothing to wait for."

"Okay...is it a good deal?"

"Based on my research on the web, it's the best one I can find in southern California. I wanna get it."

"Okay...let's do it!" I was so excited that she agreed. She knew that this was important to me, and her support meant the world.

As I told the salesmen I wanted to purchase it, I told him the story. I told him that over a year ago I left my wife and ended up in a psych hospital where I had a vision...a mental picture of me driving a black Mercedes down PCH with a blonde in the passenger seat. As I told him that I wanted that blonde to be my wife who I had reconciled with, tears began to form in his eyes.

He couldn't believe it. He couldn't believe that he was selling a car because of a psych hospital vision. He couldn't believe that my wife was willing to take me back.

Within the same week, I drove off the lot with the black Mercedes Benz I envisioned, and I purchased plane tickets for our entire family to go to India for Christmas.

I couldn't believe what I was experiencing.

A year and a half ago, my life was an absolute wreck. I walked away from my incredible family and a wonderful church that I had invested my life in. I hit rock bottom, landed in a hospital, and then fought for my life for several weeks.

Through a great deal of counseling and forgiveness, my wife was willing to take me back. Laura got a great job, and I was running a marketing business that was giving us the financial opportunity and the time to go to India. We had a small community of Jesus-followers who were supporting us in our endeavor to start a children's home on the other side of the globe. And, I was driving off the lot with a beautiful Mercedes.

That drive down PCH with the blonde in the passenger seat was absolutely wonderful. It was a moment of freedom and responsibility. I had the freedom to enjoy self-expression and creativity while developing an intimate relationship with the love of my life, and I exercised responsibility by making a financial decision that fit within our family's budget.

Maybe my buddy Ron was right.
Maybe life was going to be even better than before.
And, maybe I was going to be more successful than ever.

The only difference was that success now didn't look like building a big church. It was more about loving God, developing an intimate relationship with my family, and enjoying the freedom and creativity to use the gifts that God had given uniquely to me.

Christmas in India
On December 20th, 2009, we boarded the plane for the biggest "Trotter Family Adventure" to date. With our two, elementary-aged kids in tow, we began a journey that would change our lives.

Although I had been to India six or seven times, Laura and the kids had never joined me. With great courage, we were heading to the place that had captured my heart for those of the lowest caste. We were heading to visit the children's home we started in partnership with Harvest India just a few months prior. We were heading to where I had started my relationship with Samantha.

The potential for healing was tremendous…and so was the potential for disaster.

The week before we left, it hit me all at once. Having just gotten my new car washed, I was driving down Lincoln Avenue in Cypress when I looked to my left and saw…the Peacock Motel. The place Samantha and I spent our first night together after getting back from San Diego. I wasn't pulling in to the motel with a backseat full of black trash bags with my clothes inside them. Instead, I was driving home to my wife and kids who had been willing to walk through the fire to reconcile with me.

I was now living the life that I truly wanted.
I was married to a wonderful partner.
I was loving my kids.
I was enjoying using my gifts and talents to serve others.
I was developing new friends who were coming into my life.
I was at peace, and I was making a positive impact in the world.

On the first Sunday after our arrival in southern India, I was scheduled to preach in a little village that I had been to on several occasions. In fact, I had spearheaded an effort at Revolution Church to fund a church building and a concrete home for the pastor's family…rather than the mud-floored, thatched-roof one they had been living in for over 20 years.

The last time I had been there was in 2008 with Samantha and the rest of the team. During that trip, we dedicated the pastor's home, and they honored me with the biggest flower lei I had ever seen and a hat so large that it rivaled the one worn by the pope.

Now there with my family…we walked across the bridge and entered the village, I was reminded of the inner turmoil of that night almost two years prior. I wanted to sit with Samantha, but she was nervous and practically pushing me away. My heart was completely ravaged by my strong emotional connection to her and the simultaneous accolades by the village for our work on the church and home. I could feel the dissonance within my soul, and I was miserable.

This time…it was completely different.

An elderly man in the village had passed away that morning, and we were ushered into the confines of the family's stick fence surrounding their mud hut. The dead man was laying in the dirt with cotton in his nose and a leaf in his mouth…some sort of Hindu ritual. With my kids sitting wide-eyed next to me, I prayed for the wife and all the surrounding adult children as the smell of burning incense wafted through the air.

After touring the pastor's home so that Laura and the kids could see the work we had accomplished, we entered the small church with leis placed around our necks. As I stood up to speak, I knew that I had to be honest. I knew that I needed to confess.

"Two years ago, I sat outside this building while we dedicated your pastor's home. You honored me for our work, and I was humbled. I want you to know that two weeks after I got home, I made a horrible decision…I left my wife."

With permission from Laura, I confessed my selfishness to the pastor, his wife, and their congregation. I talked about the opportunity that God had given me to start over…a second chance at my marriage and family.

"I was dead, but I'm alive again. I was lost, but now I'm found." I told the small congregation as they sat on the concrete floor.

Being the last Sunday of 2009, I invited them to join me in looking toward new opportunities that God had for all of us in the new year.

"There are new opportunities that God has placed right in front of you.

Some of us have blown it in huge ways in the past, but our God is a God of second chances. He is a God of forgiveness, grace, and new opportunities. Are you ready to take hold of the new opportunities that He's bringing into your path in the next year?"

I sat back down in the white plastic chair on the stage, and I hesitated to look over at Laura. I didn't want to see the pain on her face. Other than the night of our vow renewal event, this was the first time I had shared my story publicly with her present.

I gave in and looked to my right.

Laura's eyes were filled with tears. She didn't look angry...just sad... sad for all the brokenness and loss and pain over the past two years. As our eyes connected, I felt closer to her than ever before. In my complete weakness, she was willing to show me love.

I looked to my left, and Suresh and I smiled at one another...both us knowing that things had come full circle. Once again, I was inspiring people to live a great life...not out of a need to perform or be successful in some way...but out of a depth of brokenness that knows my full need for Divine Love and Grace.

> *Amazing Grace, how sweet the sound,*
> *That saved a wretch like me.*
> *I once was lost but now am found,*
> *Was blind, but now I see.*

My story didn't have to go this way, but these were the choices I made.

It took me getting lost
to finally be found.

AFTERWORD

by Laura Trotter

I never thought I'd have
to worry about my husband cheating on me.

We seemed to have such a good marriage, and we rarely even had an argument. We built a great life together…two beautiful kids, a wonderful home, and a church that loved and supported us.

I could see that Dave was getting burned out as a pastor, so I listened intently and wanted him to feel less stressed. Unfortunately, it only seemed to intensify as the years went on. He was running so fast and pushing so hard, but I had no idea this could happen. When he went to India in February of 2008, I had no idea that he was going to hit a breaking point. I didn't realize that things would never be the same.

Living through an affair and then choosing to reconcile is the hardest thing I've ever had to face.

The truth is I was completely shocked when he came home from India and told me he was *done* with our marriage and ministry. It felt like I was blindsided in a 'hit and run' accident, and I was pinned down and unable to break free from the other car. I couldn't even move.

On top of that, the other woman involved was one of my closest friends. Our kids hung out together, our families went camping with one another, and we enjoyed several date nights together with our husbands. We connected either in person or via phone several times a week.

How could she do this to me? My brain couldn't compute how this could be happening. I was devastated that she would choose to leave her family and our friendship for Dave.

To make matters even worse, the affair was quite public. As you read, Dave made the choice to leave his whole life for this new adventure with her. It was incredibly painful to know what was going on every day...just a mile from our home in their newly rented apartment. I feared that the kids and I would run into them at any given moment.

I was devastated, and the pain seemed endless.

As I look back over the last few years, there are so many things that I have learned through this experience...

1. I had to focus on a daily routine to help us survive.

In the face of tragedy and loss, I forced myself out of bed every single day so I could teach 25 kindergartners and distract myself from all the pain. I knew it would help my own kids to see me getting out of bed and functioning like their *normal* Mommy. Although *nothing* was normal, I had to do everything within my power to keep them comforted.

We were going through so much, and routine was key to helping us all survive.

2. I immediately started seeing a therapist and my doctor.

As soon as Dave returned home from India, I knew things weren't looking good, so I made an appointment to see a licensed family therapist. Week after week, she helped me sort through all my feelings, and she listened as I grieved the decisions Dave was making. I felt it was important to take care of myself regardless of what he was doing. I had to survive this trial whether we stayed together or not.

Because of my anxiety, depression, and weight loss (25 pounds in one month), I also made an appointment to see my primary care physician. I shared with him what I was going through, and he prescribed several medications to help me cope with all the pain and encouraged me to start drinking protein shakes to prevent further weight loss.

No matter what Dave was choosing to do with his life...I had to focus on *my* health and the health of our children.

3. I relied on God for daily strength and hope.

There's no way I could have walked through the pain, loss, and tragedy of this entire experience without my faith in God. The daily strength and hope that God provided was immeasurably more than I could ask or imagine.

Every day, I was sustained by a still small Voice who would comfort me with words of hope. I knew I wasn't alone. I knew God would never leave me or forsake me. God was willing to walk with me through all this pain, and I had the opportunity to trust Him with the outcome.

4. I began to address my own personal issues.

Although Dave is completely responsible for the decision he made to leave our family, I soon realized there were patterns in *my* life that contributed to a lack of health in our marriage. Rather than simply blaming everything on him, I took stock of my own life and started aggressively looking at what I could learn from the situation.

As I read "Torn Asunder: Recovering From an Extramarital Affair" and worked with my therapist, I began to experience so much growth in my own life. Once again...whether Dave and I were ever to be together again or not, I wanted and needed to become a healthy woman on my own.

5. I was open to seeing transformation in Dave's life.

When Dave called me and asked meet on May 3rd, I didn't know what to think of his request. Their affair had ended two weeks prior, and he spent three days in a mental hospital.

As I sat across from him at a park, I felt numb from all that had occurred over the past two months. Although I could see his brokenness, I was thinking, *"It's about time you apologized to me. What took so long?!?"*

I was thankful he didn't ask me to take him back, and I was encouraged to hear that his main goal was to get his life together and get healthy in every way. Frankly, I didn't think there was much hope for us at the time.

How could we move forward after such a horrific chain of events? I couldn't see anything beyond making it through the next day.

6. I chose to reconcile with Dave because of his genuine remorse, authentic life transformation, and a commitment to our family.

I prayed long and hard about what I was supposed to do with the whole situation. Our divorce was already in motion and would have been final in a couple of months.

Not only would I have to adjust to being single, but I'd be forever connected to Dave because of our kids. Even if I didn't want him to be around, I would have to share our kids with him...including holidays and some weekends.

Divorce sounded so hard, but reconciliation seemed even more painful. I couldn't fathom how we could work through all the issues in our relationship. I didn't know if it was possible to overcome all of the pain he inflicted on the kids and me.

Yet, after observing his behavior for several weeks, I could see a transformation taking place in his heart. Not only was he willing to let me vent my frustration, anger, and pain without feeling a need to respond, he was investing focused time and attention in our kids in a way that was completely different. I could see he was ready to commit to our family in a new way.

That's when I decided that it was time for us to go to counseling to start working on our relationship. Over the next couple of months, I made the decision to reconcile with Dave as I saw tremendous changes in his life.

The road to recovery from the affair has been long and painful, but there has also been amazing growth in my life and in our marriage. As you can imagine, it has been a wintery season of life for me, because of so much loss...the loss of being part of the church we started, the loss of close friendships, and the loss of all that once was.

I have chosen to embrace the sadness and continue working through it all so I can fully heal. I have chosen to work toward forgiving Dave and my friend for the decisions they made, and I have chosen to consistently forgive people who slandered us and even cut us out of their lives. I have chosen the path of forgiveness as I leave hatred and bitterness behind.

I appreciate the people who have been able to walk with us during this time of healing, change, and recovery. From my fellow teachers who walked with me daily to the new relationships in New Wine Community to reconciled friendships with people we haven't connected with over the past few years...I'm thankful for each and every one of you.

Painful experiences and tragedies will arise during different seasons of life. I now know that I can allow it to make me bitter and cynical, or I can embrace the moment and trust God will use it to transform me into an even more beautiful woman.

I'm choosing to embrace my beauty in the midst of brokenness.

END NOTES

[1] Kimya Dawson, *Loose Lips*, Remember That I Love You, K Records, 2006.

[2] The Moldy Peaches, *Anyone Else But You*, The Moldy Peaches, Rough Trade, 2001.

[3] Chris Tomlin, *The Way I Was Made*, Arriving, Sparrow Records/sixsteprecords, 2004.

ACKNOWLEDGEMENTS

Laura

Thank you for your undying support as I wrote my story…and throughout our entire marriage. I am inspired by your courage to lean in to challenging situations and allow God to transform you in the process. You are my passionate and adventurous wife and partner, and I love parenting our children with you. I'm so thankful for your forgiveness. I love you.

Waverly & Emerson

Although I loved you when I was the "old Daddy," I'm so thankful for the opportunity to experience life with you as your "new Daddy." I look forward to every single day with you…from singing in the car as we drive to school to watching Brady Bunch under the red blanket at night. I love you more than ever.

Mom & Dad

I am grateful for a wonderful heritage and loving family. The stable, God-honoring environment in which you raised me has provided a compass that helps me align my life. Your love for me is clearly evident, and I truly enjoy spending time with you. I'm glad that God chose you to be my parents. I love you both so much.

Suresh Kumar - www.harvestindia.org

Your words of wisdom and grace mean far more than you could ever know. You have truly shown me what it means to love the least, last, and lost...I have been one of them. You are my Indian brother, and I am thankful that you have chosen to walk with me.

Randy Powell - www.journeyscounseling.com

You have an unbelievable way of speaking into my life, and I'm grateful that God nudged me to seek you out once again. Thank you for being willing to kick my butt and love me...all at the same time. Your gift of wise counsel is remarkable.

Keith Page - www.rockbottomministry.org

Thank you for your incredible investment within me over the years. God used you in the darkest time of my life to save me. I'll be forever grateful for your listening ear while I was lost, your wise counsel as I sought to re-connect with Laura, and your forgiveness along the way.

Kevin & Kim DeAllen

Your deep love and devotion to me are truly appreciated. You took me under your wing and allowed me to be part of your family when I couldn't be with my own. Thank you for your incredible friendship.

Darren Clowers

I know that God aligned our paths to cross at just the right time. He knew that you would be willing to be 'with' me when I desperately needed someone. Thank you for your difficult questions that spur me on to think about what (and who) I truly want in this life.

John Weeks
I only needed one person to believe in me when I sent that email offering my services…and you were the one. Thank you for responding positively and giving me a chance. I love our friendship…the world travels, the laughter, and the insanity. You are a confidant that I deeply trust.

Rick Mysse
You invested in me and protected me over the years more than I'll ever know. Thank you for being a 'rock' when the waves of ministry were crashing around me. And, thank you for your grace.

Stacey Robbins - www.staceyrobbins.com
What a pleasure it has been to work with you as my writing coach! I can't think of anyone else that I would have rather worked with in this process. I love that Laura and I could trust you with my story and this experience. Thank you for all the thought, prayer, and encouragement.

Chris Koble
Thank you for reaching out to me when I felt all alone. I'll never forget our first dinner together after my life imploded. Your listening ear and heart of compassion were so needed. I value our friendship so much.

Jon Gaw
Our journey has included many twists and turns, but I'm so glad to be walking this road with you. I appreciate how you challenge my thinking and call me to a higher place. Your friendship is invaluable! I love you.

New Wine Community
What a gift to have a small community of faith develop among a rag tag bunch of Jesus-followers who have gone through such painful life transitions. We deeply appreciate your love and support along the way.

Revolution Church
Although I wish I could say this to you face to face, I deeply regret my selfish decisions that caused such great pain and damage to you. My repentance is to live a new life that is honoring to God and to my family. May God continue to bless you as a community of Jesus-followers.

For more resources by David Trotter:
www.nurmal.com

To contact the author:
www.davidtrotter.tv